TRINITY AND ALL SAINTS
A COLLEGE OF THE UNIVERSITY OF LEEDS

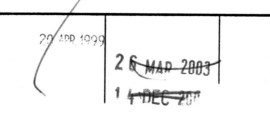

LIBRARY

This book is due for return on or before the last date stamped

20 APR 1999	2 6 MAR 2003	
	1 4 DEC 20	

WITHDRAWN FROM LIBRARY STOCK
LEEDS TRINITY

GETTING
THE BEST OUT OF
PEOPLE

GETTING
THE BEST OUT OF
PEOPLE

David Robinson

Published in Association with
The Institute of Chartered Accountants
in England and Wales

KOGAN
PAGE

For William, Edward and Caroline

Copyright © David F Robinson 1988

All rights reserved. No reproduction, copy or transmission of this publication
may be made without written permission.

No paragraph of this publication may be reproduced, copied or transmitted
save with written permission or in accordance with the provisions of the
Copyright Act 1956 (as amended), or under the terms of any licence
permitting limited copying issued by the Copyright Licensing Agency, 7
Ridgmount Street, London WC1E 7AE.

Any person who does any unauthorised act in relation to this publication may
be liable to criminal prosecution and civil claims for damages.

First published in Great Britain in 1988 by
Kogan Page Limited, 120 Pentonville Road
London N1 9JN

British Library Cataloguing in Publication Data

Robinson, David F.
   Getting the best out of people.—
   (Business enterprise guides).
   1. Manpower planning   2. Personnel
management
I. Title   II. Institute of Chartered
Accountants in England and Wales
III. Series
658.3′01   HF5549.5.M3

ISBN 1-85091-532-6
ISBN 1-85091-529-6 Pbk

Photoset in North Wales by
Derek Doyle & Associates, Mold, Clwyd.
Printed and bound in Great Britain by
Biddles Ltd, Guildford.

Contents

Introduction

There are few subjects more mysterious than people and what makes them tick. The old Lancashire saying that 'there's nowt so queer as folk' with its implication that people are quixotic, irrational, unreasonable and so on is amply borne out by most people's personal experience. And yet a manager is charged with the task of keeping his subordinates enthusiastic, loyal, hard working and motivated, while simultaneously fulfilling his other numerous duties. It's not surprising, then, that many managers and individuals setting up businesses look for help and guidance from management specialists as well as from fellow managers – after all, they're only human.

Books on managing people seem to come in three styles: some suggest that a few simple rules (in some cases 'tricks') will ensure a happy, obedient workforce, who will follow the smiling, perfectly adjusted, manager to the ends of the Earth. Others offer models of complex organisations that are almost impossible to relate to the experiences of the 'typical' manager. And then there are textbooks of personnel management and behavioural science and the like which the layman is simply unable to comprehend.

This book tries not to fall into any of these categories. It offers a simple, straightforward introduction to the main topics with which every manager should be familiar if he or she is to get the best out of the people reporting to him or her. It deals with the failings and foibles of employer and employee alike in familiar contexts and it is based on over 20 years of advisory experience with organisations of every size and type.

Getting the best out of people is always hard: it is always an imperfect activity and there is always more to learn. However, without some element of success in this aspect, a manager will neither satisfy his or her personal goals nor those of the organisation.

The benefits of getting the best out of people in business are as rewarding as the penalties are dire. Those who ultimately succeed are those with the personal qualities and skills which enable them to command the respect and support of colleagues and subordinates. The manager who fails is usually consigned to the outer darkness of the organisation, to some 'limited damage' role of lowly standing and influence. The founder of a new business who fails to succeed in his 'man management' will almost certainly be condemning himself to remaining a perpetual 'small business'.

Can these skills, attitudes and techniques be learned or is there some magical chemistry of personality, time, place and opportunity which opens the door to the chosen few? Well – there is no management alchemy which can turn base metal instantly into gold. Happily the machinery of business, government, the academic world, organised religion and any other activity in which people work together towards a common goal requires not gold, but metal of more common availability. For the great majority, a combination of sound intelligence, keen observation and a willingness to learn with good guidance should improve management performance by a marked degree. It is the purpose of this book to provide such guidance and to help the manager to achieve both greater success and satisfaction from his or her job.

The text is structured in topic-related sections following a carefully chosen sequence, designed to deal with the major concerns of any manager in handling people. Practical examples have been included to help illustrate the text. Appropriate reference is made to technical sources where this is needed and a selected reading list is provided for those who wish to investigate topics in greater depth. Above all, the book aims to be readable and interesting to a wide variety of individuals ranging from the student of management to the mature manager in an established position.

To avoid unnecessary clumsiness in the text the word 'manager' is intended throughout to include both male and female holders of that office and the same applies to other generic terms such as 'leader', 'entrepreneur', 'proprietor', 'subordinate' and so on. Similarly, from here on, the word 'he' is used for simplicity but should be taken to apply to either gender. (A section is included in Chapter 6 which deals with particular issues of discrimination and ethics faced by women.) The word 'subordinate' is used, reluctantly, in view of the lack of any satisfactory alternative. To some people it implies too subservient a relationship which is apparently out of sympathy with much of what is best in modern management. However, the manager's job is to direct individuals reporting to him in carrying out their duties. To this extent, at least, the word 'subordinate' is both apt and wholly accurate, and so has been exclusively used throughout the text.

This book is not a personnel management textbook (you will not learn how to design management by objectives forms from it), it is not a homily (we are all learning after all) and it is not a series of personal anecdotes. But hopefully, this book *will* be both entertaining and useful to you.

1

The Challenge of Effective People Management

The most valuable resource

If you asked the owner of a small business what his most valuable asset was he would probably say, 'The factory ... the stock ... the machine tools ... the goodwill.' He would be unlikely to say, 'My staff' because convention dictates that the human asset is not valued. As the owner of a successful advertising agency put it, 'They go down in the lift at night and with luck, they come up again in the morning!'

It is self-evident that, without the human factor, profit, wealth creation, enterprise and all the other good things which make organisations successful, would not occur. The human resource is the magic ingredient which turns raw materials, lumps of metal, empty buildings, money and the like, into products, commerce and happiness. This factor is even more important in those organisations which provide services to the community – hospitals, schools, local authorities, and so on.

Few organisations take time to add up how much they really invest in their employees. How much it costs to recruit them (advertisements, agency fees, interview time etc), to train them (formally and at 'Nellie's elbow') to pay for their mistakes while they are still learning the job, to reskill them when the product or the technology changes, to counsel, advise and direct them when they have problems, and to persuade them to stay when they are determined to leave. Some organisations *have* done the sums and the totals are startling. Thousands of pounds for typical new entrants to an organisation and tens of thousands for more senior people. A necessary part of the cost of being in business, of course, but a neglected investment.

If an organisation made an investment in computers equivalent to that made in its staff, the time and effort which would be spent on making sure that they worked efficiently would be considerable. A financial payback would be demanded and performance carefully monitored against the original plan. Inquests would certainly follow failure to perform.

Surprisingly the same rigour is seldom applied to making sure that investments in people achieve an adequate payback. Indeed it is almost universally true that small organisations pay no real attention to it all. This is perfectly acceptable when the overall objective is being more or less achieved. For example for a small company, newly formed, the first priority is survival. Like a new-born baby the enterprise fights for life, owner and staff dedicate every ounce of energy to this one end with uncompromising commitment. The questions of whether or not the human resource is well or badly used, whether people are contented or discontented, adequately managed or not, are thought to be irrelevant. This assessment of the unimportance of man management is not only wrong, it can be terminal for a business on the margin of survival. In the same way that a new business needs to demonstrate how its physical and financial resources are to be deployed, thought and planning should be applied to the management of its people.

As organisations progress from the early, critical stages of survival into young maturity when the focus changes to efficiency, the need for good man-management techniques become even more self-evident. Unfortunately, many growing organisations stumble and stagnate at this stage in their history because either this need is not recognised or the means to satisfy it are unavailable. Good people are often lost at these times, disillusioned perhaps with unfulfilment of early promises, and the inherent investment in them (including their knowledge of the enterprise) has to be replaced.

Whatever the size of the organisation, be it a new enterprise on a science park, a multinational corporation or a metropolitan teaching hospital, the people are their most valuable resources, and getting the best out of them should be of paramount importance. Making sure employees are well housed, adequately paid and agreeably occupied is demonstrably not enough. They must also be well led and well managed.

Management – science or art?

Many aspects of management have been conveniently reduced to principles and rules which the dedicated student can learn and apply.

The management of people is, however, not amenable to this approach and there are no infallible rules to follow. However, relying on instinct and good luck is just not enough.

The reasons why managing people can't be reduced to simple, scientific, procedures are not difficult to see:

- every person at work has a unique character, set of skills, attitudes and weaknesses;
- every group of people working together will behave differently from every other group because of the individuality of those in it;
- every manager is different and hence so is his relationship with the people he manages;
- each application of the management process is under unique circumstances.

Using a simple analogy it is rather like playing on the same golf course every day – the course remains the same but the combination of conditions, shots and golfers' proficiency makes every round unique.

Good man management can be helped by understanding some fairly straightforward guidelines and adopting techniques for diagnosing particular situations. Large corporations apply such 'scientific' training techniques to executives taking on their first managerial appointments and turn out reasonably competent debutantes. Small companies seldom, sometimes never, apply any systematic approach to meeting this need and rely on recruiting management talent into their businesses.

Even after training in the basic skills few would claim that they are anything more than beginners. The reality is that the 'art' of man management which turns the raw beginner into the mature expert cannot be learnt from management textbooks. It is substantially a combination of:

- working with good managers and learning from them;
- analysing his working environment and the behaviour of colleagues and himself;
- making and learning from his mistakes.

There are few better tutors than a well-disposed colleague who is not only a good manager but can also explain clearly why he does things. This is often a problem in small organisations which are usually founded by people with little managerial experience themselves. The input of management expertise needed by those companies can sometimes be made by non-executive directors. Sadly, many such companies ignore both the need and the solution. The message for the aspiring manager is simple – try to learn your craft in an environment which employs good managers.

The issues to which analytical techniques need to be applied are explored in this book. Some case-study material also illustrates the types of problem which can result in management failure. But the techniques are no more than paints on the manager's palette, and the picture which he produces must be wholly his own.

Managing people is a combination of science and art – science in the standard, systematic, procedures for personnel management and art for handling the vast diversity of human organisation and individual behaviour.

Changing management needs

Managing people is not difficult – it's just extraordinarily hard to do well. The degree of severity of the task depends on three key variables:

- how rigid is the structure within which management takes place;
- the characteristics of the people to be managed;
- the skill of the manager.

All these can vary not only between organisations but over time within the same organisation. For example, the man-management needs of an army with a strongly established command structure change as the average educational standard of the new recruits improves. Technicians working at computer terminals have to be handled differently from the semi-skilled labourers they replaced. Managing people well in a travel agency needs a different approach from dealing with workers in a car plant.

In general terms, the more highly regimented the structure the more the manager can rely on his rank to carry him through. In totally unstructured situations true management talent is needed. *The Admirable Crichton* is a play in which the roles of an Edwardian gentleman and his butler are reversed when they face survival on a desert island. The gentleman can no longer rely on the social order to support his position and the skill of the butler makes him the natural leader of the castaways. Nowadays there are fewer and fewer organisations with structures in which it is the job which is respected rather than the jobholder. Man-management skills have never been needed more.

For the growing organisation, and particularly newly formed young companies, there are several distinct stages through which the development of management skills normally pass before a mature and stable condition is reached. Many of these stages are painful, can be extremely prolonged and, in some cases, prove terminal to the business.

Five growth stages are illustrated in the following table:

Growth Stage (Approx no of employees)	Management focus	Management style	Man-management approach
Venturing 1–10	Survival	Charismatic	Vision driven
First plateau 10–50	Efficiency	Personal/informal	Individual
Emerging Professionalism 50–250	Growth	Personal/formal	Departmental
Second plateau 250–500	Security	Organisational/formal	Company wide
Mature growth 500+	Strategic vision	Professional/personal	Strategic

NB. The number of employees is indicative only and will vary considerably according to the nature of the business. Growth stages for public sector, charitable, academic and similar bodies do not follow this pattern.

In the *Venturing* phase the leader of the business demands total commitment, the priority is survival and the whole team will work night and day to achieve it. Man management is seen as being of no relevance by those running the business.

A *first plateau* is reached when the business clearly *will* survive and the emphasis moves to profitability and efficiency. The management style is still informal and man management emphasises the needs of the individual.

If growth continues a stage is reached when informal methods break down and *professionalism* emerges, usually signalled by key appointments such as qualified engineers, accountants, research managers, and so on. Formality of management style follows and the man-management approach focuses on departmental concerns.

A *second plateau* is reached and is comfortably occupied by many medium scale organisations. The business is preoccupied with preserving its markets and profits and adopts styles and man-management approaches which are 'company wide'. Many organisations find at this stage a relatively stable balance between the feeling of a corporate community and the need to have well organised and managed personnel systems.

The final stage of *mature growth* is achieved when the focus of the organisation changes to a strategic vision which leads to a management style in a new personal, but highly professional relationship with its staff. At this stage the man-management approach also becomes strategic. Career planning, training and personnel, and organisation development are the priorities for the personnel function.

Few managers see that company through all these phases. Those who do, know that the worst times are not when you are squarely in one of the stages but in transition from one to another. Achieving a smooth transition is not only an accelerator to growth but an enormous credit to those managers who see it through.

The manager's skills

The manager either takes on a role in an organisation he knows well or joins one with which he is less familiar. He will certainly have some idea of what is expected of him and the nature of the people he is to manage. If it is his first management job, he will be less sure how best to concentrate his effort and what sort of problems he will encounter. It's a lonely and daunting prospect.

The manager in this first post will face a special difficulty – the 'lance corporal' syndrome. He will be a small step only above his staff in terms of authority. If he has previously been one of their group he will find it very hard to impose discipline on them. If he tries to be tough he risks ridicule, if he is too soft his role will be ineffectual.

Young managers need discreet but attentive support from their superiors during this testing period (usually lasting only a week or two). The superior should be around to endorse the manager's most difficult decisions – being in the background at a critical meeting is often enough to show that the manager's authority is real and not nominal. Another crucial need is for systematic training in basic personnel techniques such as:

- conducting interviews;
- keeping personnel records;
- carrying out appraisals;
- assisting with pay reviews, promotion decisions and disciplinary matters.

In this early stage it is highly desirable for the new manager to have a mentor within the organisation. This person should be a more experienced manager or, in a small company, the owner. Leaving a new manager to get on with it unaided is inexcusable.

After two or three years' experience the manager should have gained the basic skills of handling people and should be ready to progress to the next stage. Through training the manager should be equipped with the ability to:

- chair meetings;
- develop and administer effective job descriptions;
- handle sensitive personnel negotiations.

Managers at this stage in their careers can also benefit from training which gives them a better understanding of their own motivation and behaviour. Such courses, which are often run on group counselling lines, help to temper the confidence gained by that stage with a sense of realism. Learning from others at the same point in their careers is a crucial part of this process. This is often difficult for small companies to arrange on their own, but can be done on a cooperative basis with similar firms.

The manager's progress after perhaps another five years should see him as a director of a small company or a departmental manager in a large one. His training needs now centre on such skills as:

- time management;
- delegation;
- personnel planning;
- communication skills.

The likelihood of his getting this sort of training very much depends on his organisation's perception of management needs. Sadly, experience suggests that small companies disgracefully neglect the training of their top management. It is somehow thought to be a sign of weakness for a director to do anything so mundane. Strangely, one-day courses on topics such as 'Going to the USM' or '101 Ways to Save Tax' are always over subscribed by such people. They seem to be unaware that learning a really useful skill, such as effective time management, has a continuing effect for the rest of their careers and is a true investment in the human resource!

More senior management appointments in large organisations often involve the use of extensive support from trained personnel professionals. They inevitably deal with much of the routine which the manager previously dealt with himself. His new skills have to include using such services while still retaining a close personal relationship with his team of immediate subordinates. The needs of the manager at this stage of his career are complex and very much depend on his personality. Entrepreneurs who succeed in building large companies often find the challenge of delegating effectively and relying on highly expert professional managers extremely difficult to handle. They tend to veer between irrational favouritism and deep suspicion of everyone's motives. The result is unsurprising – deep insecurity for all involved!

Self-assessment

Throughout this process of personal development the manager must regularly check his own progress. How should he do this?

With any luck the manager is the subject of a well-run appraisal system which gives him a periodic view of his strengths and weaknesses. In small organisations these are rarely very well developed and the manager has to rely on self assessment.

The best way to tackle this is to ask some key questions.

Effectiveness
Is the team achieving its tasks regularly, calmly and effectively? If not, how much of the failure is accountable by management mistakes made by you?

Team spirit
Would the team put itself out to handle some particularly unusual or difficult task? If not, why not?

Morale
Do the team enjoy their work, meet outside working hours, laugh spontaneously in each other's company? If not, how much is this due to your attitudes and management style?

Individual motivation
Are the members of the team usually motivated to give their best to the job in hand? Are they ambitious for promotion? If not, are you failing to lead them adequately?

Crises
Have you had any confrontations, rows, sullen acceptance of your decisions, slammed doors, resignations and other storm warnings? If so, who else is to blame but you?

Your own job satisfaction
Do you generally feel relaxed, on top of the job and enjoy the challenge of managing people? If not, find out what's wrong – and put it right!

The manager can also test his own attitudes by rehearsing situations in which, for example:

- he has to choose between applicants of equal ability but of different sex or colour;
- he could cover up a management mistake by blaming it on his boss or admit it openly to his team;
- he has to declare a long standing and faithful employee redundant.

Situations such as these may well occur in practice, but in their absence the manager has to imagine what he would do and study his own reactions. These mental 'gymnastics' are an essential part of the manager's learning process. Indeed much of good man-management depends on being able to imagine what *might* happen if a particular course of action is pursued.

Experience

Formal training, self assessment and the advice and counsel of other managers all have their part to play in the learning process. But the best teacher is experience, assuming that the manager understands and learns the lesson offered by the event.

This is not as certain as you might imagine. There are man managers who 'protect' themselves from the learning process by explaining away their failures in terms of:

- the weakness/myopia/stupidity of their own bosses;
- the weakness/myopia/stupidity of their staff;
- divine intervention or any other cause except their own inability or error.

This failing is frequently compounded by the reluctance of colleagues or superiors to correct the repetition of the mistakes. For example, a manager may infuriate his staff by spreading gossip. This indiscreet behaviour doesn't directly affect efficiency, but it disturbs trust between individuals and lowers morale. The problem is that no subordinate will raise the issue with the manager and run the risk that this will, in turn, be gossiped about. His own boss in all probability is unaware of this weakness. If the manager fails to be self-critical he will continue the behaviour, will not learn from his mistakes and will probably see no connection between this and subsequent resignations from his team.

Gaining experience depends on handling events and problems

outside the normal pattern as well as dealing with the day-to-day routine of working life. Such events are likely to involve:

- confrontation between individuals (one of whom may be the manager);
- disciplining individuals for unacceptable performance or behaviour;
- sacking someone;
- confronting another manager or his boss on some matter of principle affecting his staff;
- advising an employee on a serious personal problem.

The possibilities are legion but the approach should be the same. The manager should always both review the outcome of handling such problems and make sure that he learns from the experience. Many managers fail to take the time to do this and, in consequence, never progress in their chosen discipline. Small companies often employ very adequate but idiosyncratic senior personnel whose management training has been totally neglected, whose foibles are tolerated but whose personal needs for development have never been explored or attended to.

The challenge

The manager has responsibility for one of the organisation's most valuable resources – its people. The context within which he is asked to meet the challenge of management will vary from the highly structured to the chaotic. His own training and experience may be very limited and the opportunities for seeking the help of colleagues non-existent. Most of all, he has to learn about himself and attempt to overcome the weaknesses which might affect the effectiveness of his management. In combination these factors can seem overwhelming. In compensation, the job satisfaction involved in being a good manager, however small the team, can be enormous. That is why so many cheerfully take on this task. They accept the challenge as a true test of all aspects of their character.

2
Leader or Manager?

The question posed in the title of this chapter is of fundamental importance to all organisations. In young enterprises the difference in the roles is usually academic since they are combined in one person – the founder. As the organisation grows, roles become more defined, and understanding the respective contributions they can (and should) make to getting the best out of people becomes crucial.

Unexplored territory

While there are numerous books on management practice and principles, there is little more than a handful of useful works on leadership. This suggests, correctly, that the subject is a tough one and it would be foolish to suppose that all its complex facets can be captured in a short book such as this. None the less, understanding the fundamental activities of the leader (as distinct from the manager) and the dilemma which all leaders must resolve, is an essential part of getting the best out of subordinates. The reason for this is simple. Communications between manager and subordinate can be in a variety of different 'tones'. The 'tone' of the leader is essentially different from that of the manager. For example, when Churchill called for 'blood, sweat and tears' from the British people in 1940 he was speaking as a leader, not as a manager. He did not literally expect an immediate and public sacrifice, nor did the audience expect to provide it. But when he wrote instructions such as, 'Pray send me this day appropriate intelligence regarding our coastal defences' the recipient could have no doubt that a prompt reaction was expected!

In practice, the leadership and management messages transmitted to subordinates by a boss are often more confused (and confusing) than the simple example of the words of an acknowledged leader. This confusion leads, in turn, to unexpected and sometimes unwelcome

21

reactions. In young companies employees compensate for this confusion by understanding that the entrepreneur must both inspire and direct. As such companies grow, however, the clear and separate functions for leadership and management are likely to suffer increasing problems, particularly during the transition. These problems can gravely inhibit the smooth growth of the organisation. This can be best illustrated by a case study.

The new branch

Alan has established a successful offset litho plate processing business. Starting on his own he soon recruits two young men – one to handle sales, administration, despatches and the like, and the other to deal with all the technical angles. Alan himself covers all roles as needed but is particularly keen on winning major accounts, catching the headlines in the local paper and looking for ways to expand the business. The three young men work all hours, meet most evenings in the pub after work and share a common enthusiasm for the business. However, Alan is clearly the 'boss' and his authority is not questioned by the other two. He pays them well and gives them bonuses to reflect good results, but does not share profits or business risks with them. They are a happy team.

Alan briefs his colleagues informally on all relevant developments in the business and they share together hopes and worries for the future. In particular he explains to them his plans for opening up a new branch in a nearby town. The way he puts it to them is, 'If things go really well I think we can expect to open a satellite in the new year. We shall need to appoint a really good chap to run it of course – and within a year or two it will be turning over £60,000 or so ...' Alan's colleagues enjoy the excitement of shared planning and the feeling that the 'we' he referred to is a genuine team. Their enthusiasm for Alan and his business drive, and their confidence in him as their leader is unbounded.

Alan, however, emitted misleading signals. He knows that his new branch will need a manager with talents which neither of his existing colleagues possesses. He is reluctant to disturb a settled and well motivated team and, in particular, to risk losing one of his valued staff should the new venture fail (an eventuality never discussed openly). In consequence, when the time comes Alan recruits a manager through an employment agency and proudly announces his new appointment at one of the trio's regular soirées. He is taken aback when the reaction is hostile, petulant and highly personal. Perceiving deep disloyalty in his colleagues Alan complains bitterly to his wife that the reward for involving people in your thinking about the future is to have everything thrown back in your face in a very insulting way. All in all the cause of good 'interpersonal relationships' takes a knock from which it will take a long time to recover.

Simple analysis would demonstrate to Alan that sharing plans and strategies for the future with subordinates – a vital part of leadership – carries with it obligations to explain the rules of the game. Alan's colleagues saw the sharing of the plan (leadership) as part of a continuum including putting the plan into action (management). Alan's failure to put his comments into a frame of reference led them not only to assume that the consultation process was bound to continue through all phases, but also to have expectations of early promotion. This mixing of messages at different levels and with different implications is one of the most common faults of inexperienced entrepreneurs.

Simple rules

In this example Alan could have avoided the difficulty if he had observed some simple rules:

- always make it clear when you are dealing with strategic issues;
- explain (or reinforce) the role of the audience in the discussion;
- describe how management decisions will be made in implementing policy.

In practice Alan could have said, 'My plan is that when the time is right, we shall open a branch ...', 'I shall want you to help me to decide when it will be commercially sensible to start looking for a property ...' and 'I will recruit a new man as manager since you have a more important contribution to make here ...'. All simple and perhaps obvious statements, but essential to avoid the potential confusion surrounding these 'leadership' statements.

So, what are the leader's essential tasks and how do these relate to his responsibilities for man management?

The leader's role

The leader's primary task is often that of setting medium- and longer-term objectives for the enterprise and ensuring that adequate resources are available and properly deployed to achieve them. In small organisations the objectives may be relatively modest: 'to make a living for the owner', for example, or 'to become the major supplier of cut flowers in the town'. In large and complex organisations the

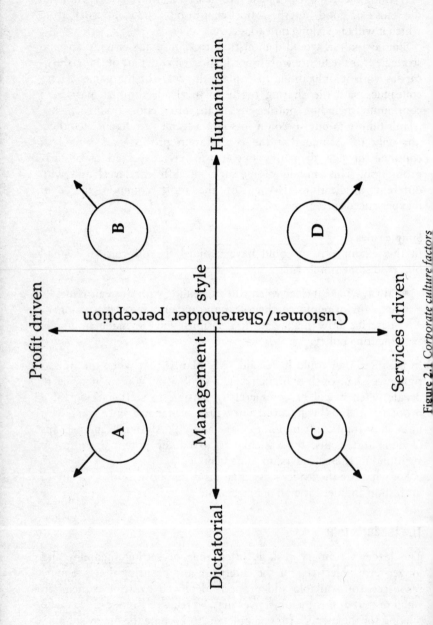

Figure 2.1 *Corporate culture factors*

process of setting objectives and reflecting them in adequate statements often involves huge amounts of corporate time and money. The value of the effort put into this apparently simple task is reflected in the cohesion with which the organisation subsequently works towards its commonly stated goals.

This objective setting task has an essential element which may be described as setting the 'tone' or 'culture' of the organisation. Getting this right is not as simple as might at first appear. The reason is that there are many corporate styles which can be adopted equally validly within any given environment.

Choosing the right culture
The problem is to choose the best option.

The two axes of the diagram represent the organisation's management style on the one hand, and the customer/shareholder's view on the other. The scale on the axes is irrelevant – what matter are the implications of positioning the organisation in each of the four segments.

An 'A' positioning would suggest a culture giving financial results pre-eminence, and concern for the interests of the individual low priority. The nearer to the 'corner' point A moves, the more extreme these pre-occupations would become. Everyone knows 'hire and fire' companies, who care naught for people's feelings or their careers, and pursue only maximum profit. Paradoxically, dictatorial, profit-driven organisations seldom get anywhere near profit maximisation since the system involved creates enormous resistance from employees. (Organisations in primary industries and in less developed countries are often exceptions.) Few leaders would set out to position their organisations in this segment.

A 'B' positioning gives profit generation high priority but puts increasing emphasis on human values in the way the organisation is managed. At the 'corner point' the organisation would attempt to reconcile 'benevolence' with profit maximisation. Opinions vary as to whether these objectives are compatible in practice. There are some notable examples of very successful companies which give high priority to their 'caring' attitudes (avoiding redundancies, encouraging co-ownership and profit sharing, offering good fringe benefits for the employee and his family, and so on). They tend to be found in industries servicing relatively stable, long-term markets (food manufacturing, retailing, textiles and the like) with in-built employment patterns not susceptible to fashion or short-term change. Doubtless such companies benefit from the morale building effect of caring policies on corporate loyalty and willingness to accept change. In some companies, however, the cost of too much caring could be crippling (not many record companies would want to keep ageing rock stars on the payroll until they're 65!). Many leaders choose cultures positioned in this segment because the combination of profit seeking with humanitarianism is appealing both inside and outside the organisation.

A 'C' position gives customer service high priority (for example running unprofitable air routes to complete an otherwise partial network) but with a highly directive management style. Many public service organisations operating as bureaucracies fall into this segment. Some will argue that being service driven and being profit driven are not mutually exclusive objectives. Indeed, if the organisation is a supplier of simple, uniform products, attention to customer service may well be the key to profit optimisation. The great majority of organisations, however, have to recognise the need to reconcile profit and service objectives. For example, a shoe manufacturer almost certainly loses money on sizes 3½ and 12, but has to provide them to secure customer credibility. Few leaders outside the medical business, the academic world or the transport industry, for example, would want to associate their corporate culture with this segment of the chart.

A 'D' positioning is epitomised by organisations with charitable or humanitarian aims. There is a clear tendency for many commercial enterprises to attempt to achieve high service levels, humanitarian management and acceptable levels of profitability. It is part of the leader's job to decide, in the particular environment within which the organisation must work, whether such disparate aims can be reconciled.

The task of the leader in choosing and imposing an appropriate culture for an organisation is hard enough for a new enterprise. It is doubly hard when a new leader inherits an organisation with a style and culture which are not working successfully.

Policy priorities

Having made the choice of culture, the leader's next job is to establish in the organisation the structures and policies by which it will be maintained in practice. They can be identified under a number of straightforward headings.

- *Organisation structure*. The jobs and relationships between different people in the structure have to be defined. This topic is examined in more detail in Chapter 4, but when viewed from the

perspective of the leader the structure chosen should be:
- appropriate to the service needs of the organisation;
- efficient in operation;
- robust in terms of accommodating changes resulting from both internal and external causes;
- consistent with and reinforce the chosen culture or style of the enterprise.

Within this structure the leader needs to define his own role in relation to the rest of the management. Typically, in established commercial companies the chairman's role is distinguished from that of managing director (or chief executive) largely on the principle of separating the leadership tasks from those of day-to-day management. In practice much of what occurs in the decision-taking process involves committees and, as discussed below, setting up appropriate structures for those is another element in the task.

Small or newly formed organisations often avoid the issue by not explicitly defining their structure at all. The argument that 'everyone covers for everyone else's job' and that 'team spirit would decline if we put people in boxes' are usually offered in justification for this lack of formality. It is certainly true that there are advantages in keeping arrangements flexible in young companies so that the best structure can emerge from practical experience. Undue delay in defining and organising a structure can, on the other hand, have disasterous results in terms of efficiency and morale. When in doubt it is better to install a clear structure (and be prepared to change it) than to wait for some unforeseen event such as the loss of a key member of the team to precipitate it.

- *Decision taking and communication structures.* The organisation structure will deal with the authority levels of individuals ('The store manager can authorise credits of up to £100', for example) and this will provide the skeleton for the working organisation. The flesh on the skeleton is the structure which the organisation employs collectively to make decisions, and to communicate both vertically up and down the organisation, and laterally across it. These structures almost invariably involve committees (excepting the one-man business) and their role, contribution and authority must be defined if man-management processes are to operate well. In larger organisations specialist committees may be charged with, for example, considering strategic issues (supporting the leadership function) and personnel and human resource issues (supporting the man-management function). Whatever structures are chosen, their method of operation and decision-taking powers must be set by the leader.

- *Personnel policies.* These include such items as pay and rewards policies (who gets a company car, for instance, or who is entitled to be in the share option scheme), appraisal and promotion criteria, training policies, disciplinary procedures and so on. For small organisations much of this is inevitably informal. But whatever the size of the organisation the leader needs to keep a sharp eye on personnel matters since they lie at the heart of getting the best out of people.

- *Key team members.* The leader must personally pick the key senior people to run the organisation. In small businesses, where the owner both leads and manages, this problem does not arise. In large and complex enterprises on the other hand, the choice of the right management team is crucial. The leader must also monitor the performance of this team and be prepared to step in and insist on remedial action if he is unhappy with the way things are going.

The leadership dilemma

In leading the people in the organisation and getting the best out of

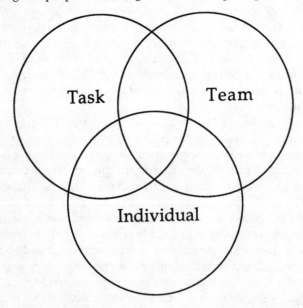

Figure 2.2 *The leadership dilemma*

them in terms of efficiency and enthusiasm the leader faces a dilemma.

The 'Task' circle represents the commercial or service goals of the organisation for which the leader is responsible. The 'Team' and 'Individual' circles represent, on the one hand, the general interests of the employees of the organisation (and in particular its management) and on the other those of any one employee. These three elements are often in conflict. A typical case will illustrate this.

Conflicting needs

The chairman of a toy company decided that the only way the firm could prosper and grow was by abandoning traditional products and specialising in electronic games. He knew the consequences of this decision were substantial redundancies, a reorganisation of the board to bring in new skills, and the early retirement of two senior directors. He had to reconcile:

- what was essential for the business (the strategy change); with
- the dramatic effects on employees (the team consequences); and with
- his responsibilities to two loyal board colleagues.

His analysis of what he should do included examining the likely effect on the others of getting the *best* result for one element at a time.

If he made the hard-nosed commercial decision he reckoned that he would not only lose his early retirees, but also his managing director and several other key people. If he concentrated on what was good for the team, minimise the effects of change and avoid redundancies, the commercial consequences could be dire. If he acted to protect the jobs of his board colleagues, both the commercial objectives and the team's health could be jeopardised. In the light of this the chairman chose to make a less radical process of change to get the commitment of key people to supporting the process and make sure that the counselling needs of the two retiring directors were fully met.

Leadership styles

The illustration shows that leadership is usually not about choosing between straightforward alternatives, but complex and subtle ones. The leader must not only convey his judgement to others but make sure that action follows the formulation of policies. The execution of policies is the manager's job and the leader's relationship with the manager varies according to the needs of the organisation and his capability level. The leader can:

- direct
- counsel
- coach *or*
- guide

according to circumstances. The more expert and mature the manager, the less directive the leader needs to be. A distinction should be drawn, however, between the leader's responsibilities for strategies and policies and the manager's job to carry them into action. The skills needed are very different and it can't be assumed that the leader can, for example, coach the manager in all aspects of his job. Many a good entrepreneur is a bad man manager. Expert handlers of people, on the other hand, regularly lack the innovative spark needed to make fortunes and found business dynasties.

What makes a good leader?

The qualities that go to make up a good leader are many and varied. There is no recipe which can guarantee success in leadership since the best leaders are determined individualists. This emphasis on personal qualities means that many leaders see their role solely in terms of realising their own ambitions. In the short term this approach clearly has merit, but often fails in the long term because the *skills* of leadership have to be learned and practised over a period of time. The armed forces have long recognised the need to have not only a good method of spotting leadership talent, but also a continuing and comprehensive programme of training to develop the associated skills.

Small companies are often destined to stay small because the person with the initiative and leadership qualities to get them started cannot progress beyond the approach which worked in the founding phase. This has little to do with commercial flair or organising ability, but a great deal to do with handling people.

What qualities and skills does a leader need?

- *Vision*. The leader must be able to identify and communicate to his colleagues his vision of the objectives of the organisation. In young businesses these may be very simple – grabbing some market share from a competitor, making a better engineered product, offering an outlet for some new service, etc. As businesses grow their objectives become more confused and the leader's job consequently becomes harder. If he consistently fails to remind his colleagues of the vision and its attainability, loyalty, morale and motivation will progressively weaken and, eventually, fade away altogether.

- *Judgement.* Very difficult to define or measure but a quality which certainly separates the good leader from the bad. A surprising amount can be learnt formally about the way in which decisions are made at top level. Successful leaders often spend a lot of time collecting information and opinions before drawing conclusions. The idea that success depends on immediate and determined decisions is fallacious.

  Judging the qualities of his subordinates, encouraging and directing them to make the best of their opportunities, is another important virtue in a good leader. It is a real challenge for strong leaders to attract and retain really capable colleagues rather than mere ciphers or 'yes' men. Sadly many fail and their enterprises collapse through lack of strength.

- *Energy.* Leadership is an exhausting activity physically, intellectually and emotionally, not least because the leader dedicates his whole being to the pursuit of his beliefs. Despite his high consumption of brandy and cigars, Churchill clearly had an astonishing capacity to sustain long periods of activity when his colleagues were wilting. Stamina is therefore an important part of successful leadership.

- *Determination.* Leaders are more prone to suffer setbacks in their careers than managers because they are often breaking new ground and taking risks. The abilities to bounce back from disappointment, to keep on banging away at an idea when surrounded by sceptics and not to take 'No' for an answer are essential. Although the quality is partly inbuilt in the person, much also depends on the social environment (in the USA failure is seen as part of the learning process) and personal circumstances (wives, husbands, friends and family often contribute enormously to the leader's self-confidence).

- *Consistency.* This is the acid test for many leaders. The ability to lead and inspire others very much depends on predictable attitudes, philosophies, loyalties and decision-taking methods. Many leaders, intoxicated with the success they achieve, forget this elementary message. In organisations which grow rapidly, the leader's relationships with his senior colleagues is often destroyed by his variability and inconsistency. When businesses have shared leaderships (such as in partnerships) the problem of retaining consistency is particularly acute. There are many man-management skills and communications which the leader can acquire by recognising and responding to a training need. Sadly, in many organisations nobody points out these needs to the leader if he fails to see them himself.

- *Fairness*. What may be 'fair' in dealing with people will vary. The important thing is for the approach to be consistent. For example, if the leader is known to expect a certain level of performance from his managers as a condition for them keeping their jobs it is more important that the rule is consistently applied than whether or not it is fair. The most difficult man-management problems facing a leader are to do with the competence of senior people. The fairness with which he is seen to deal with such problems has a considerable effect on morale and loyalty of the people working for him.

- *Ruthlessness*. Leaders must act quickly and ruthlessly when necessary. The needs of the organisation must always come first and the decisiveness with which the leader acts gives very strong signals both internally and externally about the health of the enterprise. Ruthlessness does not necessarily equate with inhumanity or insensitivity. The moral code or ethical standards of the leader form an essential part of his influence over the organisation which he leads. If they are regarded by the bulk of his employees as being reasonable his actions will usually be judged in a favourable light.

- *Self-knowledge*. Many leaders are irrational, eccentric and egotistical to such a degree that they appear incapable of progressing beyond fanaticism. While such qualities may be the stuff of politics and revolutions, they can be fatal flaws in a leader's intent to inspire long-term confidence in commercial organisations. The ability to understand his own actions and motives, to assess his own strengths and weaknesses, to trade off success and failure alike is an important part of a leader's make up. Self-knowledge is not the same as introspection, and the process is private and personal. (Public self-examination is usually taken to mean indecision.) Very often the leader has a confederate with whom experience is replayed and problems worked out. Non-executive directors or strategic consultants fill this role in larger organisations – spouses and partners in smaller.

- *Skills*. The leader must be a good *communicator*, he must also be a good *listener* when it is needed. He should be able to *set* and *monitor standards* of performance of the organisation and to *make decisions*. He should know how to *encourage* and to *reprimand* when needed. Last, but not least, he should know when to interfere in management and when not to – in a word how to *delegate*.

The manager's role

The manager's role is different from that of the leader. Even though the jobs are often combined in one person in small organisations the distinction between them is of fundamental importance.

The manager's task is to be both *effective* and *efficient*. His performance must be measured both at the individual level (how good he is at his own job) and the team level (how well his contribution supports the achievements of the organisation in which he works). Managers need a wide range of skills, of which getting the best out of people forms only one part. It is, however, an extremely important aspect of his job and, in many environments, such as those with significant creative content, it can be crucial to the success or failure of the enterprise.

The manager's role in man management can be divided into three aspects:

- dealing with his superiors;
- dealing with his equals;
- dealing with his subordinates.

Handling the boss

Newly appointed managers often have problems in coming to terms with this part of the job. Sheer gratitude at being given the responsibility to look after some part of the organisation can overshadow the need to develop a mutually acceptable relationship *upwards* in the hierarchy as well as *downwards* in it. The manager must find the most effective *modus operandi* with his boss within:

- the circumstances of the organisation;
- the individual working styles of the two people involved.

If the organisation lays down rules for every aspect of the manager's job and specifies in similar detail the boss's role and responsibilities, the scope for upward influence is limited. But such organisations are extremely rare because few people are willing to be regimented to such a degree. In most organisations the act of appointing a new manager, however junior, affects the whole structure in some way. It also presents opportunities for new management initiatives to be taken by both manager and boss.

The boss-handling task of the manager falls into three aspects:

- understanding and exploiting the boss's preferred working style (is he a 'one-minute manager', is he an avid memo writer, is he a 'soundings taker'? and so on);
- reflecting the needs of his own team in terms of communications with the boss (demonstrating the support for the team's interests and concerns);
- being sensitive to the boss's own position in the organisation, the strengths and weaknesses of his role and the 'political' dimension of his activities.

All good managers attend to these needs in such a way that their bosses (if they are also good managers) approve of and encourage the process. This does not mean that the manager avoids conflict or differences with his boss, rather that the relationship is based on mutual understanding and respect. Respect for the boss must be reflected in his respect for his subordinate. Without this the relationship is one of master and serf. Surprisingly often, the initiative taken by the subordinate establishes the tone of the relationship rather than vice versa.

Dealing with equals

The manager has no specific responsibility for getting the best out of his colleagues except in those rare instances where a design or project team operate as a peer group. None the less, successful managers can clearly be distinguished from their less successful brethren by the way in which they handle, and are esteemed by, their equals. Most organisations would expect a manager to be 'a good team man' pulling his weight in his particular specialisation but contributing equally to the team effort: a highly laudable aim but one which bears little resemblance to the realities of life in most organisations!

The essential features of how to handle equals well are simply stated. The manager needs:

- *territorial recognition*. He must not only recognise the patch occupied by his colleagues but also respect the conventions involved in dealing with them (however weird and wonderful they may seem to be).
- *non-aggression treaties*. The manager's motives, ambitions and political intentions must be clear and unequivocal and mutually

understood (particularly when criticism is involved); this avoids suspicion, personal resentment and vendettas.

- *operating protocols*. By which the manager consults, shares decisions and advises his colleagues; these may be laid down by the organisation (for example the committee structure) or be evolved by the manager and his colleagues on an informal footing.

Not treading on toes

In a fairly typical business, a manager may want a fellow manager to grant him a favour. For example, the sales manager might want the production manager to rush through a particularly urgent order. Going through the official chain of command via the sales director and the production director will take time and has no guaranteed outcome. In any case the sales manager wants quick results, so what does he do? He telephones the production manager (we'll call him Dave) and:

- chats about Dave's favourite sport/pastime ('How are the pigeons?');
- shows that he recognises how busy Dave is and how impossible is his request ('I know it's probably out of the question ...');
- makes his request in such a way that he signals his recognition of Dave's authority ('A word from you would bring it to the front of the queue ...');
- offers reciprocation ('I'll see if I can get that German order rescheduled ...').

Dave knows full well that the sales manager could use the hierarchy if he chose. He also knows that he is being handled according to unwritten peer group laws and will comply if he can with the request.

This type of informal 'trading off' between equals is a vital ingredient in all businesses. If the myriad day-to-day problems which beset all managers were not soluble in this way, most organisations would grind to a halt. This is true whatever the size of the organisation but the smaller the firm the greater the cooperation needed between individuals. As a result the opportunities for misunderstanding and friction are much greater. Most people with experience of working in a small team know how easy it is for people to fall out over trivial matters. In many cases the issues involved are ones purely associated with status and authority. People get easily put out if they think they are being:

- taken for granted;
- bypassed;

- handled discourteously;
- manipulated or brow beaten by an equal.

This is sometimes classified as touchiness or a 'prima donna' temperament. Often it is neither, but rather a breakdown in those subtle and informal understandings between equals which make for flexibility and ease of communication across an organisation.

In summary, relations between equals are fraught with potential risk if mishandled. It is an essential part of the job of the most senior manager in the organisation (the managing director or his equivalent) to direct and guide these peer-group relationships to ensure that they work in the best interests of both the individuals involved and the organisation.

Dealing with Subordinates

This task is likely to occupy the great bulk of the manager's time. The role requires the manager to:

- *assign tasks* to subordinates – the term 'delegation' is commonly used and is often assumed to involve transferring responsibility to the junior person. No amount of delegation alters the manager's personal responsibility for everything that is done within his team and the expression 'task assignment' is consequently more accurate and apt. The skill with which he matches the job to the ability of the subordinate is an immediate indicator of the manager's quality; good task assignment avoids favouritism, encourages personal development and rewards individual success.

- *support, coach and direct* individuals in his team in carrying out their assigned tasks. This activity is much influenced by the experience and skill of the subordinates and the difficulty of the jobs they are asked to do. The manager has to apply his time in a way which offers the greatest payback in terms of results from the team. This sometimes creates problems where, for example, the pace of one individual's work slows down the rest of the team. Problems such as this are discussed later in the book.

- *reward and reprimand* individuals as necessary for their performance. Reward is often expressed in terms of praise and recognition (rather than simply monetary reward). The psychological value of this type of reward is discussed in Chapter 4. The ability to reprimand in a way which offers a positive stimulus to improve performance is one of the manager's essential skills.

- *care for and foster* the needs of individual team members. This involves knowing them on a personal basis and being sensitive to their attitudes, prejudices and priorities. This does not mean that the manager has to be 'one of the boys' or pry into the private lives of his staff. It *does* mean that he should be perceptive enough to spot potential anxiety, stress, rebellion, disenchantment or alienation in a subordinate and deal with it on a personal basis. In small organisations this is usually not difficult for the aware manager. It is much harder where the organisation is large or geographically dispersed.

What makes a good manager?

The man-management tasks described above sound relatively straightforward and easy to perform. If the manager's personal standards or those of the organisation for which he works are undemanding it is true that modest attainment will suffice. If the manager is going to get the best out of his people he will need to show appropriate personal qualities and technical skills.

Earlier in this chapter, the qualities required in a leader were described as being:

- vision
- judgement*
- energy*
- determination*
- consistency*
- fairness*
- ruthlessness
- self-knowledge.

The manager needs some of these qualities in greater measure than the leader (those marked * in particular, but in the context of executive decisions rather than forming policy). In addition the manager should have:

- diplomacy
- communication skills
- organising ability.

Diplomacy is an important attribute because the manager's judgements are often concerned with resolving conflicts between the requirements of the task and the resources available. This often leads to the manager having to make what appear to his subordinates as compromise decisions. The manager must be able to negotiate, persuade and influence decisions both within his team and in other parts of the organisation. Abrasive managers may be feared and respected for their short-term achievements but they rarely succeed in the long term. Diplomatic handling of man-management issues does not imply 'softness'; indeed the hardest messages can be conveyed just as effectively with tact as with tactlessness. The vague term 'maturity' is often used as a synonym for this most important quality in a successful manager.

Communication skills are vital if the manager is to develop and sustain successful relationships with his team. Some managers communicate most effectively in writing, others work best orally. The manager must make sure that he spends sufficient time working face to face with his subordinates, either individually or in groups, to understand their characters. They will look to him for clear communication on such occasions. Indecision, vagueness, sarcasm or partiality will be quickly evident to the manager's team and will cause long-term damage to the manager/subordinate relationship. Few managers write as fluently and effectively as they should. A considerable training need exists here throughout all types and sizes of organisation.

Organising ability is expected of all managers but, in practice, is found in few. Most have the 'props' of the systems and procedures to disguise their inadequacy in this respect. Subordinates work best when their boss is ordered, tidy and uses his time in such a way that crises can be handled without undue stress. A good organiser is available when a major problem occurs (whether personal or business). A poor organiser destroys the confidence of his team by both setting a bad example and making them deeply uneasy about his understanding of their needs. The skills and techniques of work organisation are easily taught and managers who fail to learn them are doomed to failure in the long term. The manager's ability to delegate in turn depends on this.

Finally the manager should have both a sense of proportion and a sense of humour. It is hard enough to deal with human relations, without the dead hand of a humourless and unreasonable management style.

Leadership and management – are they compatible?

The paradox of all human organisations is that they need both leadership (with its long term horizons and missionary commitment) and management (with the emphasis on carrying out tasks effectively and efficiently). The 'proportions' of the two ingredients vary. Young companies and those going through major periods of change (markets being realigned, new technologies being introduced, ownership changing, and so on) need heavily emphasised leadership. Mature organisations, particularly those providing services and products to the community or operating on a large scale, need a predominantly management culture.

Leaders and managers are often uncomfortable partners. The Jekyll and Hyde characteristics of charismatic (but unpredictable) leaders and sound (but dull) managers are recognisable in many highly successful enterprises. The secret of their success is usually finding a practical *modus vivendi* between the two styles. Others suffer from constant turnover as managers, the mercenaries, move on to more agreeable enterprises. Success therefore depends on finding the right mix to keep the enterprise stable and moving in the right direction.

Good leaders often learn to be good managers and vice versa. Many of the talents needed in a leader cannot be easily taught but there are few management skills that a leader can't learn. Small companies often don't grow because the leader fails to separate the roles and either acquire the necessary management skills himself, or hire someone to carry out this task for him.

Personal development

Many organisations take great care to be on the look out for managerial and leadership talent, and to develop programmes of experience and training designed to exploit that potential in the most effective way. People working in such far-sighted and benevolent organisations are indeed fortunate since the development initiative lies essentially with others.

The great majority of leaders and managers and particularly those in small companies are not so lucky. For them personal development means just that – choosing to improve by taking the initiative themselves. What kind of things should such people do to improve their effectiveness?

- *Find a 'guru'.* Whether a leader or a manager it is invaluable to have another, more experienced, person to share problems and opportunities with. Such a person may be within the organisation or outside it. Business founders often have difficulty in sharing confidences with others but a sympathetic accountant or lawyer can sometimes meet the bill. Non-executive directors in mature companies can be both valuable and effective in fulfilling this function. The key is that the leader/manager should be both frank with his mentor (it's no good just giving the glossy version of events) and be prepared to listen to his reaction. Following the advice given is often less important, since actually explaining the problem can lead directly to its solution.

- *Watch others*. Observing a good leader or manager work has the most powerful potential for development if the leader/manager is willing to learn. If he is not it will simply cause envy or depression or both.

- *Read widely*. Much of what is written on management topics is ephemeral rubbish, but hidden among the dross can be found valuable insights into the management process. Books, magazines and newspapers all contain input to the manager interested in learning more about people and how they behave. Case studies of how successful organisations operate, and how companies grow and prosper are a particularly valuable component in the personal-development plan.

- *Spot the skills gap*. Draw up an inventory of the skills you need to handle people in your job (this book will help) and rate your skills against each category. If a gap can be filled by training (for example, if you have problems writing clear reports or addressing meetings) find a course and get yourself on it.

- *Assess your present job*. Review whether or not your present job offers the scope and context within which your personal development can prosper. If not, either persuade your organisation to give you more opportunity or change your organisation!

3

The Organisation – Springboard or Straitjacket?

Someone working on his own needs only to organise his own time and the other resources needed to complete the task in hand. As soon as more than one person is involved in doing anything, some form of organisation structure is needed.

This may sound like an exaggeration but examining even the simplest example will demonstrate its truth.

Everyone needs an organisation

Imagine two people charged with arranging the flowers in the local church. Between them they have to decide which of them (or both) buy the flowers, who will get the key from the verger and who will wash the vases and dispose of the dead flowers. They have to arrange where and when to meet and each expects the other to be equally reliable. This mutual reliance and task assignment has created an ad hoc organisation. Even though it may never exist (or need to exist) again after the task has been completed, it is a crucial factor at the time.

Informal arrangements such as this don't need to have all the features of the structured arrangements found in more complex environments. For instance, the hierarchy of superior and subordinate is unlikely to exist (unless one individual is particularly dominant) and the rules governing the relationship are unlikely to be written down. None the less there is a mutual understanding of what is to be done and the roles that each will play. An 'organisation' has been formed.

If the manager is to get the best out of the people working for him, it is vital that he understands principles of how organisations work. A good deal is known about the subject by academics and personnel specialists. However, they have generally failed to share this knowledge effectively with a wider audience. Consequently many organisations, and small ones in particular, continue to make fundamental mistakes in setting up and running their operations. The result can be poor morale, weak performance, high staff turnover and managerial bewilderment.

Organisation models

There are three basic models which all organisations follow in some form or another. They occur in many variants, and sometimes different parts of the same large structure can represent all three types simultaneously. Understanding how each model works is a starting point for a manager's appreciation of his own working environment.

The three models are:

- hierarchical (mechanistic)
- cluster (organistic)
- task led (matrix)

The descriptions in brackets are the terms used by personnel specialists.

Hierarchical organisations

Ask most managers to draw a picture of how their organisation is structured and they will produce something like Figure 3.1.

If they are the export manager for example, they will show their position in the structure as being in a hierarchical 'tier' with bosses above and subordinates below. The lines on the chart are intended to show responsibility and reporting relationships and to answer the question 'who is Mr Bloggs's boss?' Simple charts of this nature work well to answer such questions and that is probably why they are so popular. For most other purposes, however, they are far from perfect.

The reasons for the imperfection of the chart lie at the heart of the problem that many people have with the hierarchical structural model. A perfect hierarchy would have:

- every job totally self-contained (no overlaps between different people's jobs);
- every job totally uninfluenced by the personality and skills of the job holder;

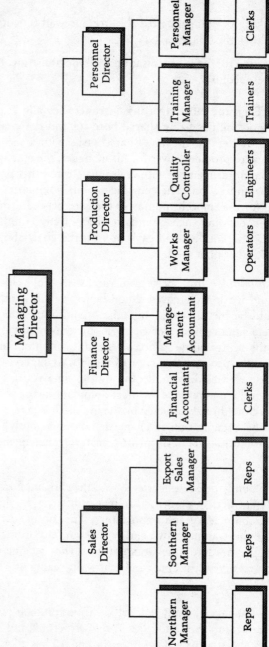

Figure 3.1 *A hierarchical organisation chart*

- every task perfectly delegated to the appropriate tier in the structure;
- no decision taking or control *across* the structure (all functions occur up and down the structure).

Elementary observation of any organisation will demonstrate the fallacy of each of these requirements.

The job boundary Even the most rigorous bureaucracies allow and provide for job responsibilities being shared both up and down and across the structure. A clerk might have shared tasks with a section leader, the section leader provides cover for his manager, the manager may be a project committee member with colleagues from other parts of the organisation, and so on. The blurring of job boundaries in practice is essential for the smooth running of the enterprise. In small or young companies, defining such boundaries too strictly could be commercial suicide. The lines around each box on the chart should therefore be blurred rather than solid.

The job and the jobholder In a perfect hierarchy the jobholder's personality, style and work preferences would be irrelevant. All that would matter would be the job itself. In some organisations this is probably true at very junior levels. For example, the personality of a private soldier in the army, or the office cleaner in a multinational company, has little influence over the scope of the job. At supervisory levels that influence becomes discernible and by the time you get to managing director level it may well be the most dominant factor of all. The structure is therefore directly affected by the individuals in it. This means, in reality, the organisation is changed, however subtly, by every retirement, promotion, recruitment or transfer at management levels.

Perfect delegation Nobody delegates perfectly and the ebb and flow of work between different tiers in the structure reflect differing levels of available resources, competence and opportunity. The job of, say, a sales manager in the illustration shown earlier will vary according to circumstances and the needs of the organisation. The tiers in the structure may reflect relative status, but rarely show the reality of what is delegated.

Decision taking Few managers, if any, take all decisions on their own. Decisions are shared both up and down the structure and by collaboration across the structure. Certainly the 'buck' has to stop somewhere but cooperation across the structure is usually a crucial ingredient in making things work. Further complications are so-called 'functional' relationships, in which one manager has some responsibility for the work of a subordinate of another manager in the business. For instance, the finance director may have functional responsibility for the accounting standards used by a costing clerk in the factory who reports to the works manager. The simple lines on the hierarchical chart, therefore, don't adequately reflect the complexities of these relationships.

Improving the model Given that most organisations are designed to have the main features of a simple hierarchy, namely:

- tiers of responsibility
- clarity of who is responsible for what
- one man one boss

how can the model be improved?

Tiers of responsibility should not be assumed to have equal importance because they are at the same organisation level. For example, people with the titles of 'supervisor', 'manager', 'director' and so on should not be assumed to have the same seniority in the organisation. Many organisations find themselves in deep difficulty in terms of pay and benefit levels because they fail either to make this clear to employees, or to create job titles to show the differentiation. They further compound the problem by omitting to note on organisation charts that 'This diagram shows organisational relationships and not levels of relative seniority.'

The details of *who is responsible for what* are not easily illustrated clearly on an organisation chart. The scope and operating style of a job can partly be dealt with in a job description (see Chapter 4). The reality of how decisions are made is an even more complex issue and the conventional organisation chart has to be supplemented by a separate 'map' if it is to be a useful guide to the organisation.

For example, the export sales manager's part of the chart could be as shown in Figure 3.2.

The shaded areas, 'Differential pricing', 'Discount policy' and so on in Figure 3.3, show typical issues which are decided in consultation with colleagues rather than by the individual alone.

TASC
LIBRARY
L R S

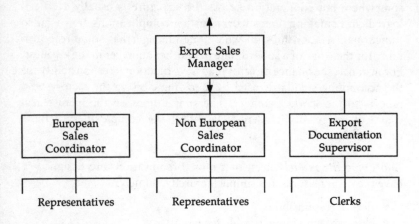

Figure 3.2 *Export sales department*

This could be complemented by a decision 'map' some elements of which would be as follows:

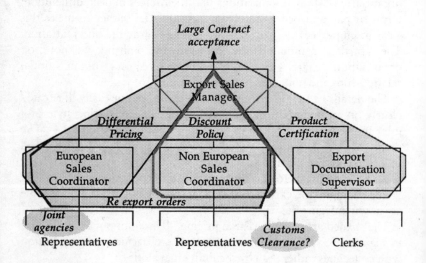

Figure 3.3 *Improving the export sales relationship*

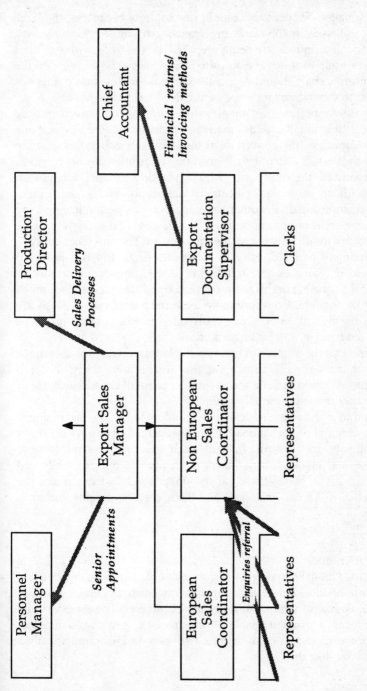

Figure 3.4 *Export department contacts*

Such 'maps' can get very complicated to draw because of the large number of issues involved. In practice they are most effectively used when job descriptions are being prepared, new staff being introduced or relationship problems being sorted out. Once again a caveat on the conventional chart should be included to make it clear that it does not purport to show the exact scope or authority level of each job.

The *one man one job* imperfection can be partly overcome by showing 'functional' in addition to line relationships. The acid test of a line relationship (the conventional boss and subordinate) is that the boss is the person who normally gives the subordinate his instructions. It is also usually the same person who decides on personnel matters such as days off, training requirements, task allocation and so on. A functional relationship on the other hand, involves one person having a say over some of the tasks a subordinate does or some of the standards to be met, but not for directly instructing that person. The difference between the two types of relationship is sometimes fuzzy and is a potential minefield if resources are stretched or if the subordinate decides to exploit the system. For this reason the hierarchical model needs as much clarity as possible. Conventionally these functional relationships are shown by 'dotted' lines. Our export sales managers chart might be improved (see Fig. 3.4) by such additions.

Once again the number of functional relationships is probably much larger than is usually shown on the organisation chart. The job description should include specific reference to all those which are of importance to the position involved.

In summary, the hierarchical model is adopted by the great majority of conventional organisations because it is perceived to have the merit of simplicity and control. In truth such structures are much more complex and involve many 'layers' wich operate both formally and informally. The better these can be understood and described, the more effective the organisation, and the managers working within it, will be.

The cluster model

The cluster model is typical of many small organisations, creative and academic bodies, and certain departments (such as design, research and development) within conventional hierarchies. The essence of the cluster is that a group of people working together group in an informal structure around one (or sometimes two) people. Diagrammatically a cluster looks like this:

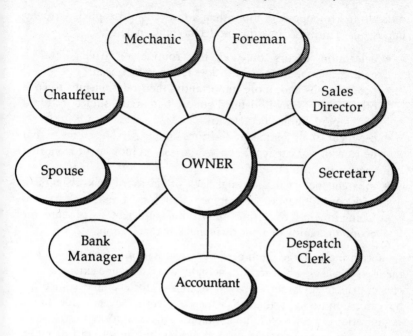

Figure 3.5 *The cluster model*

Each individual in the cluster, whatever his apparent status and task, looks to the person at the centre (in this case the owner of the business) directly for authority and decision taking. No decisions of any importance are accepted by other members until ratified by the person at the centre, and collaboration in the ring around him is conducted subject to any individual's right to appeal to the centre. Individuals move in and out of the cluster and do not even have to be subordinates in the conventional sense. Informal groupings will often occur as situations demand, but will always be capable of being dispersed at will by the person at the centre. Very occasionally such collaboration leads to someone new taking charge at the centre of the cluster.

Weaknesses of the cluster

Cluster organisations tend to be fragile, 'political', inefficient and limited in growth potential. They can prosper over short periods if the task being addressed (for example, getting a new business off the ground) is sufficiently exciting to disguise the weaknesses of the structure. Maintaining a structure of this sort over a long period is difficult and to cope with more than a few tens of people is virtually impossible. This is because this model has built-in defects:

- delegation occurs only at the routine or trivial level – management in its true sense does not therefore occur;
- people's jobs and, more importantly, their relationships to each other are not only ill defined but are potentially subject to rapid and unpredictable fluctuation;
- the focus of all significant decisions on one person can mean that he runs out of capacity, and weaknesses in judgement from that person are amplified;
- inherent inefficiency through lack of clarity of task assignment and control has to be compensated for by extra effort and 'commitment'; over time this is not sufficient to obscure the economic reality of a poorly managed organisation.

A surprisingly large number of organisations which describe themselves as being hierarchical actually work, to some extent, on the cluster principle. Owner-managed businesses, for example, sometimes have decision-taking 'cabals' to which reference is never made on the organisation chart! Not uncommonly these informal structures include a personal secretary, a long-serving but junior staff member, an ex-employee and so on. While there is nothing inherently wrong in this in the early stages, perpetuating these arrangements can prove the death knell for long-term growth.

In summary, the cluster model is commonly found but is inherently unstable and inefficient because of its informality and potential for manipulation. Employees working in such organisations need creative, intellectual or financial compensation for the frustrations and risks involved.

Task-driven structures

These structures are commonly found, and work well, in organisations where there is a significant need to man large projects with people with a wide variety of technical or professional skills. What such structures do is to create an executive relationship across what is otherwise a hierarchy to enable resources to be used as efficiently as possible in the project on hand. This means that each manager of a 'cell' in the structure has two bosses – his line manager, responsible for issues such as:

- personal development, training, promotion, salary and conditions, man-management performance;

- quality standards of work done;
- the progress of his team both as to quality and capacity;

and a task or assignment manager who:

- directs his schedule of work;
- monitors and judges his performance on the particular tasks;
- formulates and applies working methods appropriate in the project.

Such a structure is simply illustrated in Figire 3.6.

In this example each project, A, B and C has a leader whose job is to make sure that the work of the three technical 'cells' is appropriately coordinated and directed. The engineers, cost clerks and draughtsmen all have team responsibility in their own departments which would normally form part of a conventional hierarchy. This split of accountability works well if:

- the roles of the line and the project managers are clearly stated and explained to all involved;
- there is regular and full liaison between project leaders and functional managers (the dotted line on the chart);
- task requirements and resources (in both quantity and quality) are generally reasonably in balance.

Ad hoc project structures are frequently set up in organisations of all types, and as long as they have a relatively short life and are well managed, they succeed. Most organisations do not need this type of structure as a permanent feature. Those which do need special management skills.

Complex organisations

Few organisations are simple hierarchies, clusters or task-driven matrices. Elements of all three types are often found within the same organisation and further complexity is added by:

- centralisation or decentralisation (how far the process of delegation extends down the organisation);
- collectivism (cooperatives and copartnership ventures);
- impositions of law or convention specifying organisational forms (professional partnerships, trade associations, governmental bodies and so on).

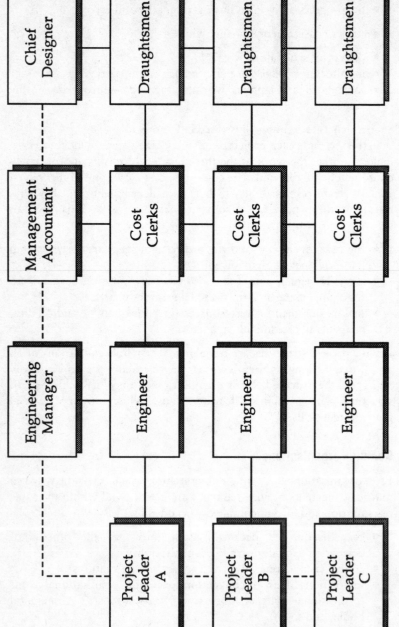

Figure 3.6 A task-driven structure

There is no absolutely right or wrong organisational type for any given situation. The test is whether the structure adopted:

- achieves the strategic objectives set for it; and
- gets the best out of the people working in it.

The more the manager understands about the reality of how his organisation actually works, the better chance he has of achieving these goals.

How organisations change

Typically, organisations change through a number of stages as they develop from foundation to maturity. The success of many organisations is a direct result of passing smoothly and quickly through these stages. Many get stuck at one stage, or misjudge or badly handle another. These factors are often more potent reasons for commercial failure than commonly quoted marketing or financial causes.

The stages involved are illustrated in Figure 3.7.

The example shown should not necessarily be taken as appropriate for all types of organisation. For example, service businesses have very different management needs from those in manufacturing. A key factor deciding when structural change is needed is how far the 'span of control' of a particular manager can be extended before things start to go wrong. The idea that there is a limit to the number of people a manager can sensibly have reporting directly to him has been accepted for a long time. Opinions differ, however, on what that number should be and much probably depends on how well organised the manager is himself. Most people would find having more than, say, ten direct subordinates a problem. In young companies, this point is often passed without the owner realising it and perplexing problems sometimes follow. Delegation is very hard to achieve in the early stages of a business particularly when many decisions could have a major effect on the success of the venture. Delegating routine responsibilities is usually the first step in the process. As more authority is delegated and lower levels in the hierarchy emerge, the progression towards a mature structure begins.

How not to handle growth
The 'Hotshot Company' is a spin off from a multinational corporation. Two research scientists, Anna and Graham, chanced on a technique for increasing the intensity of the images on visual display

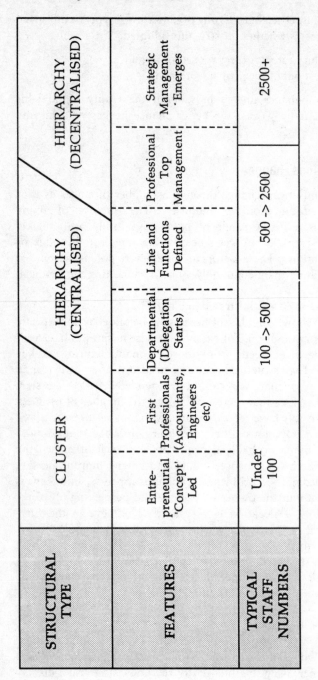

STRUCTURAL TYPE	CLUSTER	HIERARCHY (CENTRALISED)		HIERARCHY (DECENTRALISED)	
FEATURES	Entre-preneurial 'Concept' Led	First Professionals (Accountants, Engineers etc)	Departmental (Delegation Starts)	Line and Functions Defined	Professional Top Management	Strategic Management Emerges
TYPICAL STAFF NUMBERS	Under 100	100 -> 500		500 -> 2500		2500+

Figure 3.7 *Organisational change*

units, and when their employers showed a marked lack of enthusiasm for its development, they set up their new business in the smallest unit on the local trading estate. After 12 months of struggle, frustration and incredibly hard work they eventually broke through sufficiently to take on some staff and develop a proper team. New products came along, some a result of their own research, others merchanted on behalf of overseas companies, and the scale and reputation of the company began to take off. Shortly after being featured on a TV programme on young enterprises they won their first overseas order (from a major Japanese customer).

At this stage Anna and Graham had 21 employees. In addition to themselves they had 12 in the laboratory/workshop fabricating and testing circuit boards, two in the research lab, two packers/drivers, three in administration and two salesmen. The owners looked after major customers, supervising accounting and cost control, buying, shipping, advertising and promotion. The workshop was managed by a foreman also responsible for quality assurance. In any spare time, Anna and George liked nothing better than working at the bench with their research technicians on new products. Indeed, they always claimed that their first love was science and that they resented the intrusion of the business element! The fact that they were making enviable profits suggested that they were, in fact, far from naive commercially.

All was well for a time but then they started to experience financial problems. A major supplier threatened to blacklist them for non-payment. Mystified, Anna searched the office only to find that the invoices, statements and threatening letters had been mistakenly but consistently filed by the office junior. Worse was to follow. A major customer went bankrupt with the result that the bad debt not only wiped out half the year's profit, but also put them well over their overdraft limit. Their bank manager was sympathetic but firm. 'You really must get your financial affairs sorted out,' he said, 'I suggest you recruit an accountant – preferably someone with a qualification.'

Chastened, Anna and Graham took the bank manager's advice. They recruited a young accountant, recently qualified, at a salary only marginally less than their own. They decided not to make him a director – at least, not at first – but to promise him promotion when he had proved himself. Alan, the accountant, threw himself into the job and soon had the office tidy, efficient and well organised. Anna and Graham congratulated themselves on a smart move which, they felt, would help them to grow even faster. Then things started to go wrong.

The first row was over the planned computer system. Alan had looked at Hotshot's needs, researched different machines and prepared a 'board' paper for Anna and Graham. In the absence of any board meetings, Anna and Graham talked over Alan's paper one evening. The more they talked about the proposal, the more they felt that the systems which Alan would run would make him far too powerful. 'We're the computer experts,' said Anna, angrily, '*We* should decide on the machine and what it should do.' The argument which ensued was bitter and long, with Alan having to accept a compromise solution.

Next Anna and Graham had to field complaints from the workshop. They were accused of allowing Alan to be too big for his boots (he'd been insisting on time sheets being completed on time) and for spoiling the friendly atmosphere of the company.

When Alan started querying the validity of the directors' expenses things came to a head. Anna and Graham warmly reminded Alan that he was not yet a director (and wouldn't be one if he continued as he was doing) and had to do as he was told. Alan complained that they didn't understand how to manage themselves, never mind the business, and would never succeed if they insisted in constantly failing to back him. Comments became personal and Alan's resignation became inevitable. The bank manager was not amused by what he heard of the affair and decided to keep a closer watch on the company thereafter. Far from taking a major step forward, Anna and Graham felt they had taken two backwards and were reluctant to repeat the experience.

What had gone wrong? The problems of moving from an informal structure to one which accommodates management professionals had not been recognised and dealt with. The decision to take on a new man was clearly correct from a commercial standpoint. However the owners had failed to:

- consider how the new appointment would affect their roles and behaviour;
- agree with Alan what his scope of authority should be inside and outside his functional area;
- explain clearly to other staff what Alan's role was and how his work would impinge on them;
- provide a proper forum in which they could decide on issues raised by Alan.

Alan, for his part, probably failed to understand the problems he would face in moving from a very structured environment (where he trained) to an informal small company. He perhaps saw threats to his professional integrity which an older and more experienced man would have taken in his stride.

The introduction of a professional manager for the first time always causes problems of relationships with those who, having longer service, are bound to resent the newcomer. The attitude and support of the owners are crucial to this process. A hint of anything less will be seized on by those preferring more casual ways. Anna and Graham failed to grasp this and worse, saw Alan as a rival rather than a valuable colleague. Despite the excellence of the products and the people in the business, their mishandling of a crucial growth issue was a real setback.

Management orienteering

If you are the leader of an organisation, whatever its size, you have a crucial role in shaping its structure. If you are merely a manager within it, and especially if you have just joined, you have to find out where you fit in.

Understanding every facet of your own role is an essential ingredient in getting the best out of the people working for you. If you are unclear about your authority and job, they will equally be unclear about theirs.

This process of orienteering is aimed at establishing where the manager fits into:

- the formal structure; and
- the informal structure

of the organisation.

The *formal structure* is usually embodied in large organisations in:

- organisation charts;
- job descriptions;
- manuals and handbooks.

In small organisations a job title indicating rank (supervisor, manager, director, and so on) is often as much formality as is offered.

Well documented structures have a much greater chance of success than those which aren't. Even cluster organisations benefit from recognising and recording the fact that authority is highly centralised. Formal information is enormously helpful to the manager in finding his way around. However, there are some serious caveats. The manager should ask:

- is the information reasonably up to date? (Out of date information can be worse than useless.);

- is this structure endorsed by top management? (Or is it simply a recruitment aid?);
- are 'job descriptions' used for performance appraisal and promotion decisions?

If the answer to any (or all) of these questions is 'no', it's likely that the informal structure is the one which really matters.

The *informal structure* is the set of unwritten rules, conventions and precedents by which the organisation works. All organisations have informal structures to some degree because it is impossible to reflect accurately in formal documents all the nuances and complexities of a living organism. The manager therefore needs to understand how this informal structure works, and in particular how it affects his relationship with his staff.

The way to find this out is to watch the organisation at work, and to ask appropriate questions of 'old hands'.

Who decides what?

Real authority in many organisations lies with quite different people from those shown on the organisation chart. Informal 'cabals', managing directors' 'kitchen cabinets', and powerful alliances pursuing a common interest are not unknown at top levels in large organisations. At more junior levels habit, precedent or the residual influence of some long-retired office holder can lead to managers finding that, for instance, 'You can't do that without the sales manager's blessing', or 'Mr Jones always decides who gets a Christmas bonus.' Finding the real boundaries of his authority is what is important to the manager. Challenging those boundaries and the rationale behind them is a different matter.

What is the culture?

Finding out what are the acceptable and unacceptable forms of behaviour in the organisation is a key to understanding its culture. Some stress the macho work ethic, others conservatism and prudence, some businesses emphasise innovation, while others promote customer service. The nature of the culture is less important than recognising what it is and understanding how it affects the work of the manager and his staff. The approach the organisation adopts will fundamentally affect the attitude of all employees.

How political is the organisation?

Office politics exist everywhere and can be a sign of a healthy and successful enterprise. Using the grapevine (which supplements formal lines of communication), informally bypassing individuals to sound out new ideas with others, exploiting opportunities at meetings to embarrass and discomfort colleagues are all examples of political activities which are not threatening to the health of the organisation if kept within bounds. In the extreme, politics can destroy morale, motivation and the effectiveness of an organisation. The manager's job is to understand how high the political 'temperature' of the organisation is and, particularly, to know which, if any of his subordinates is likely to act in a political way.

Defining managers' responsibilities

Describing accurately a manager's job is not a simple matter of drawing up a standard job description and saying 'get on with it'. Both the manager and his boss should accept nothing than a more comprehensive statement of authority and duties.

As a minimum such statements should cover:

- the title and status of the job;
- to whom the person reports (both for line and function);
- who are his immediate peers in the organisation (his equivalent managers elsewhere in the business);
- what committees, groups or other teams he will join;
- the limits of his authority (often expressed in terms of expenditure limits, but should include personnel issues too);
- his main duties and responsibilities (including quantifiable elements and how these will be judged);
- his other duties (such as covering for his boss in his absence);
- the working methods associated with the job (extent of travelling, internal communications, involvement with external agencies, ets.);
- how progress and performance will be assessed (including references to any appraisal systems).

The key to getting the most value from such statements is to revise them regularly and to use them to measure how things are going. Job descriptions which stay in the files gathering dust are not only useless but potentially dangerous. It only takes a new employee to miss out on some vital part of his job 'because nobody explained that I had to do it' to demonstrate this. Well managed organisations know the risks involved and the value of keeping things up to date.

The benefits

Getting the structure right (if you've the responsibility for arranging it) or understanding how it actually works (if you are a manager within it), is crucial in getting the best out of people. The benefits in terms of happier, better motivated and more efficient employees are potentially immense. The damage caused by inappropriate, sloppy or poorly maintained structures can be equally damaging. High morale is often as much a result of a clear and fair structure as of highly competent management. It is well worth spending the time and effort needed to get it right. A bad structure can be the worst of straitjackets; a good one the best of springboards.

4

Human Behaviour at Work

What the good manager needs to know

Successful managers have the ability to 'read' the characters and behaviour of their colleagues. This enables them to act in the right way at the right time and as a result to win loyalty, enthusiasm and effort from those around them. How do they do it?

Good managers study human behaviour – including their own. People's characters are formed in different ways, the interplay between their intellect and their emotions varies widely. Their capacities for insecurity, aggression, anxiety and ambition also differ enormously. With this kaleidoscope of human types what is it that gives the manager the insight he needs?

The answer lies in having an understanding of the general characteristics of behaviour and relating this knowledge to specific individuals and to the team. Plus the ability to learn from his own experience and that of others.

Why do people work?

A simple question which goes considerably deeper than the obvious answer, 'To earn enough to live on.' Psychologists have established that mental and physical activity – and work in particular – is a dominant human driving force. Some argue that it is the same set of motivators which led primitive man to hunt and fight in a tribal setting. It seems that, subconsciously, everyone has a hierarchy of needs that they must satisfy in the right sequence. The hierarchy is illustrated in Figure 4.1.

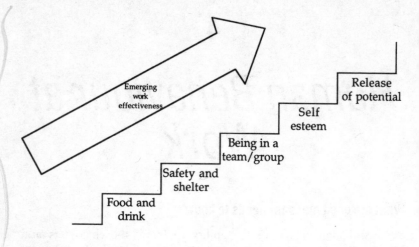

(After Maslow)
Figure 4.1 *A hierarchy of needs*

The bottom step is the survival need followed quickly by the need to have a roof over one's head. These needs usually come first and, if they are not satisfied everything else is irrelevant. Thus adequate pay and working conditions are of fundamental importance.

The next step is the need to 'belong' to some group. The family is the most elementary unit and those who are self-employed often rely heavily on the family group for support. In larger organisations it is the team, the department, the company, the trade union or the profession which may satisfy this need.

Self-esteem is a substantial part of job satisfaction and is another step up the heirarchy. It means that the individual understands the contribution needed from him and is receiving recognition for making it. Psychologists call the process of recognising and satisfying these needs 'stroking'. Words of congratulation and appreciation from a superior help to engender self-esteem. Some organisations have recently centred their management culture on achievement recognition to the extent that every correct action is rewarded by management. Initial results look impressive, but like all single-focused styles it seems likely that its effectiveness will decline with familiarity. Everyone's response to praise is different and changes with age and seniority. Reward systems need to be equally responsive to changing needs.

The final step is the *release of potential*. This may be a simple ambition to succeed, or the desire to make a contribution to a body of knowledge; it could be a fascination with solving problems or risk taking, or just a wish for the fun and companionship of working in a successful company. But fulfilment of this need is the most potent force behind a person's commitment to work. The manager should strive to create an environment in which all the other basic needs are satisfied; each individual has a unique contribution to make, and a good manager should know his subordinates well enough to make use of their expertise in a way which fulfils their potential.

Motivation

Some factors are known positively to motivate the individual at work, while others either demotivate or have a neutral effect. Motivating factors include job content, recognition of achievement, prospects of promotion, membership of a successful team and financial reward. Potentially demotivating factors include bad personnel management, poor communications, lack of clear goals, uninteresting work and failure to recognise achievement. Working conditions, the existence (or absence) of bureaucracy, and the extent to which the organisation offers welfare facilities are essentially neutral in their effect on motivation.

Most of the motivating factors lie within the power of the manager and how they should be handled are dealt with as specific topics in various sections of this book. The ones which may cause him particular problems are:

- promotion prospects (which may result from wider issues of growth and success lying outside the manager's control);
- financial rewards (because pay scales may be low or badly organised).

The manager should regularly review the effects of these factors on the motivation of both individuals and the team for which he is responsible. He should report his concerns to the level of management with power to correct the situation as part of his monitoring of personnel issues.

There are other factors both domestic (such as the trauma associated with bereavement, a divorce, moving house or a serious illness of a near relative) and work related (rivalry between two individuals, an office romance, over-sensitivity to criticism, and so on) which affect motivation. A manager cannot hope to head off these problems but should be able to recognise the symptoms and mitigate their influence on the individual concerned.

Intellectual versus emotional needs

People can be classified as being sensitive or insensitive, creative or pedestrian, systematic or careless, intuitive or reasoning, aggressive or passive and loners or team players. Personality tests are available to chart the relative score of any individual against the 'norm' for each of these characteristics. Such tests throw light on the attitudes and likely aptitudes of particular individuals. They can help the manager to achieve a better match between the individual and the job he is asked to do, and may also give an early warning of potential problems. But they are by no means either exhaustive or wholly reliable and should only be used with other relevant factors to support the manager's judgement, and not to take its place.

Whether or not personality tests are used, it is clear that everyone has a combination of intellectual and emotional needs which must be satisfied if he is to contribute to the maximum effect. It would be as pointless to allocate a highly creative, intuitive individual to a routine clerical task, as it would a systematic passive person to lead a sales mission. If the manager doesn't have the scope within the jobs available to him to match them with individuals' needs he has a problem. Although personality traits often change in emphasis with age, they rarely change completely. He is therefore faced with 'square pegs in round holes'. If the mismatch is significant he should either respecify the job (if he has the authority) or change his staff. This is not as brutal as it may seem since lasting job satisfaction is only achieved when there is a good fit between the job and the personality of the individual who does it.

Managing the individual

Most jobs in any organisation form part of a team effort. The individual is contributing his bit to the common effort and poor performance detracts, however slightly, from the overall result. In some cases the 'team' is the whole enterprise, such as in small companies. In others it may be a section, department or division.

The manager has to direct and motivate both the individual and the aggregate effort of his whole team. These two tasks call for the use of different techniques.

Assigning tasks

This is the most important function the manager performs. He must tell the individual:

- what is to be done;
- by when it should be done;
- the resources available to do it;
- his own role;
- any relevant team relationships;
- the consequence of achievement/failure.

Failure to follow these simple requirements is the most common reason for poor man management. A typical example of bad task assignment would be:

'Geoff, I'd like you to handle despatches now that Sid's left. Have a look round his desk – I'm sure you'll find the bumph you need. Give me a shout if you have problems, but not after tomorrow night – I'm off on holiday to Marbella.'

Poor Geoff! Like many willing employees, he will doubtless rise to the occasion, struggle on and hope to avoid too many disasters. How much better if the boss had said:

'Geoff, I'd like you to handle despatches now that Sid's left. I want you to produce a memo for discussion with me at 3 o'clock tomorrow afternoon covering the main aspects of the job as you see them and how they should be tackled. We can then agree on any action needed before I go on holiday tomorrow night. If we haven't got things sorted out by then, it could cause problems for Mr Palmer who's going to cover for me while I'm away.

'You'll need to look at Sid's records and probably talk to the factory and to sales. I'll call Mr Jackson and Mr Pollock to let them know what I've asked you to do. I'll also ask Michael to handle your normal work over the next couple of days while you look into this. OK?.'

Instructing, guiding and counselling

The manager has to vary his style from the terse issuing of instructions to gentle counselling, depending on the status and personality of the individual and the nature of the task to be done. Most good managers avoid the dogmatic instruction and rely on softer forms of direction. (If the building is on fire, however, there is no substitute for a direct order!)

The only true measure is whether or not the task the manager wants done is achieved willingly within the parameters he sets down. There are as many dangers in being too soft, 'If you wouldn't mind …' or 'If you could fit it in …' as there are in being too brusque '… and that's an order!' The style should be consistent, clear and respectful to the subordinate. Instructions are best given orally (a written record can follow if complicated matters are involved) since there are always a dozen ways of reading a memo, quite unperceived by the writer. Ideally, they should be given face to face rather than on the telephone. These topics are discussed further in Chapter 5 on Effective Communication.

Senior and very experienced subordinates need less instruction but probably more guidance and advice with, for example, their own man-management problems. Their priorities and work load are also matters which the good manager keeps under regular review. Every subordinate has a potential capacity to determine his own programme of work and set of priorities. Encouraging the use of these skills is vital in drawing out the individual's potential.

When giving instructions the manager should avoid confusing his subordinate by adding superfluous comment such as, 'Head office has asked us to do this – goodness knows why! More ridiculous red tape!' Whatever the manager himself thinks about the job, it has to be done – so why make it seem pointless into the bargain?

Rewarding and disciplining

Recognising good performance is an essential part of building a strong relationship between the manager and his subordinates. Recognition in private should be supplemented by public congratulation within the team when this is merited. This is a most powerful boost to the morale both of the individual and of other team members.

Reprimands are best given in private, face to face. They should not be a surprise if the individual knows what is expected of him, and should be handled simply, firmly and fairly. The most important aspect of reprimanding anyone is not the act itself but the consequences of it. The manager must ensure that the subordinate's self-esteem is not destroyed by the experience. A good technique is always to end such interviews on a friendly, personal note as far removed as possible from the business problem.

Public reprimands are almost always both counterproductive and indicative of either an organisational problem or a weak manager, or both.

Encouraging personal development

The manager has responsibility to help his subordinates to realise their potential not only in their present job but in the future. This sometimes means that the manager has to advise a rising star to move on elsewhere – a tough thing to do when he is probably an outstanding team member. A cynical approach, using any device to persuade someone to stay, may work in the short term. In the long term, however, it is counterproductive since the ruse will undoubtedly be found out by other team members and morale will suffer accordingly.

The manager who can spur on his subordinates to have faith in themselves, who supports them through difficulties and shows a genuine interest in their careers will usually have loyalty and support. In particular the manager is often the first to see the potential of the team member to acquire new skills or exploit some natural talent. Exploiting his potential with him is a mutually rewarding experience. It needs time and effort, but is extremely worthwhile.

Handling personal needs

The manager should be available to the staff member to give support in difficult times. Domestic problems can affect anyone and the manager should be able to offer a sympathetic ear. Equally, personal problems at work may need the advice and counsel of the manager. The manager may only need to listen to the problem to be giving real help, but this aspect of his work must be wholly and absolutely confidential if it is to be effective.

Managing teams

Working teams behave differently from the individuals they comprise. When a manager meets with some or all of his staff – typically, with his immediate subordinates – he has to use special management techniques.

Any meeting involving the manager and his staff, however routine or boring the purpose, has a significant leadership content. Individual staff members will be sensitive (perhaps subconsciously) to:

- how the manager deals with them (his style);
- how he deals with particular individuals (are some more or less favoured than at the last meeting?);
- changes in the manager's attitude towards the organisation or individuals in it (such as his own boss);
- changes in his attitude to the function of the meeting.

There are volumes of literature on how to handle meetings, ranging from the art of chairmanship to reading body language and other non-verbal signals. Much of the advice offered boils down to observing the same basic rules of good management which should apply throughout the manager's working day:

- *Be prepared.* Know what you want from the meeting, the likely problems and attitudes of those attending, circulate any relevant papers in advance showing what decision, if any, is needed;
- *Be attentive.* Listen and observe people's behaviour and attitudes during the course of the meeting and intervene when necessary to stop things getting out of control;
- *Be consistent.* Handle individuals in the same way from meeting to meeting using the same approach to debate and decision taking, and adopting the same management style;
- *Be rigorous.* Explore all relevant issues, ensuring that everyone has their say, conclusions are reached efficiently and actions and follow-up procedures are agreed;
- *Be brisk.* Don't allow drawn-out discussion or personal issues to fog the real business debate.

Management style

All this adds up to the manager adopting and sticking to a style which best suits him and his team. The range of possibilities can be illustrated thus:

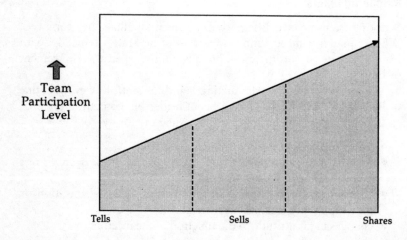

Figure 4.2 *Style of managing*

At the left-hand end of the chart the manager gives his instructions, allows questions but not debate. This is the old autocratic management style which used to be the norm in much of commerce and industry. Everyone knew their place, the 'authority of the office' was respected and any grumbling that went on was done in private.

At the right-hand end is the participative management style where the decision taking is shared with the whole team. The manager retains enough authority to have the last word but no more. This syndicated decision taking can be excellent for team spirit and morale, but can be very slow and create enormous frustration. This results from differing levels of management experience among the team members and different perceptions of the problem. Excellent as a training tool but potentially dangerous unless the manager can keep firmly in charge of the process.

Between the two is the point at which the manager secures the support of his team by 'selling' the decision to them. Good managers guide and develop the team discussion to explore and expose the rationale behind his chosen course. Giving subordinates particular aspects of a problem to investigate and report on is a typical method used to prepare for acceptance of a decision. For example, the manager faced with explaining the rationale of a decision to move office to a different town might ask subordinates to report on the financial reasons for the decision, the attractions of the new location, the effect of improved working conditions, and so on. The subsequent discussion will be both more participative and wide ranging than if the manager had simply announced the decision to his team.

There are no 'right' or 'wrong' styles – only those that keep both the manager and his team well motivated to give their best. The area within the dotted lines in the chart, in which the manager is both flexible and participative without being overly autocratic or democratic, suits most people.

An illustration will show how a manager can obtain support for his decisions. The owner of small company has decided that in future, he will have to ask his staff to take the bulk of their summer holidays in a close-down fortnight instead of whenever they choose. He knows that this won't suit some people and others might object to 'having their lives organised for them'. However, the economics of the business are such that he can no longer afford to keep it running at half speed during the summer months. Most employees are entitled to four weeks' holiday each year, plus normal bank holidays and an extra couple of days at Christmas. The owner doesn't think of himself as being anything other than an enlightened employer, but he is fearful of a backlash from his staff.

He decides first of all to prepare a careful analysis of the financial argument. He prepares charts showing the effect on the business of having all the overheads but only half the production capacity for three months of the year. He looks back to the pattern of people's holidays in the previous year and, without referring to individuals, makes a chart of how their absence affected the number of people available in each department. He also adds information on absence through sickness. This information provides a strong and graphic explanation of the background.

Next he prepares arguments for and against each of the possible solutions to the problem. He sees them as being:

- controlled holiday periods organised according to some rules such as seniority, length of service, marital circumstances or suchlike;
- enforced overtime working to make up the capacity shortfall during holiday peaks;
- a shutdown period of two weeks; or
- job restructuring to enable the workforce to be used more flexibly.

He lists the arguments simply and fairly and illustrates the potential impact on typical employees.

Finally he prepares a detailed memorandum on how he envisages the new system being introduced. This includes dates for the next two years, transitional arrangements (honouring existing commitments, etc.) and procedures for dealing with special needs. It also explains how the skeleton staff to maintain the office and factory will be selected.

He then calls a meeting. He starts by presenting the background information. Ideally he uses an overhead projector or flipcharts, but in a small group some form of handout is probably sufficient. He invites comment on his analysis, answers questions and prompts discussion. His approach should be to lead his staff into the same process of diagnosis which he went through himself.

After this phase he presents the options using appropriate aids. He stresses the equality of the different courses without expressing any clear preference. However, he makes it clear that he is not going to ask them to vote for an alternative at the end of the meeting. He has made a decision and is leading them through a logical process – that is, sharing the management task with them.

The options will undoubtedly cause lively argument. Some of his staff will be disturbed by the implications for them and their families and the owner must control the debate. In particular he must avoid appearing not to care for their welfare.

He must finally announce his decision, providing his colleagues with the implementation proposals and offering them a period for consideration and comment (on the detail, but not on the principle). If the meeting has been well handled each person attending will feel that they:

- are fully informed about the commercial background;
- have participated in a consideration of alternatives;
- understand not only why the decision has been made but also how it will affect them;
- still have scope for contributing to the success of the scheme.

This might sound a rather elaborate and manipulative way of going about what many companies might otherwise regard as being a fairly routine matter. If the potentially damaging effects of mishandling such an issue are considered, however, particularly on a small business, the benefits of doing it this way can be appreciated. Good man-management is as much about thorough preparation and a sensitive understanding of other people's needs, as it is about management techniques.

Meetings with senior colleagues

The manager meeting with senior colleagues has the same needs for good and consistent handling as his own team do. If such meetings result in decisions which need to be communicated to his staff, the manager has a special responsibility to make sure that the timing and method of communication are agreed. There is nothing worse than an important decision being 'leaked' or announced to one group at a different time or in a different way from another. Part of the job of the chairman of the meeting is to make sure this aspect is dealt with after every decision is taken.

The manager can find himself in a difficult situation if he disagrees strongly with a decision taken by a committee of which he is a member. However, he should handle with great care the extent to which he allows private disagreement to affect his attitude to the organisation as a whole. If he always 'keeps mum' and simply toes the party line on all issues he may well lose the confidence of his staff and be regarded as a 'yes' man. On the other hand if he advertises his position on every issue he could be contributing to weakening the confidence of his staff in the hierarchy.

Having to accept decisions with which you disagree is part of the job. The skilled manager makes sure his staff understands that sometimes he needs to compromise without losing their loyalty and enthusiasm. The dilemma this causes for the manager is discussed fully in Chapter 6 on the Ethics of Managing People.

Spotting changing needs

The needs of individuals and groups constantly change. Organisations succeed and fail, new people join, others resign or retire or get promoted, people marry, divorce, have children and everyone grows older.

Change can be gradual, or it can be very rapid and potentially very dangerous in terms of morale and motivation.

The manager should keep his finger on the pulse of his team so that he can take steps in good time to correct anything that is going wrong. How does he go about it and what does he look for?

Using formal occasions

The manager should use the formal occasions of contact with his staff – task assignment, discussing results, trouble shooting and so on – to run a quick check on:

- their attitude to their work and to their colleagues;
- their motivation towards the task in hand and their enthusiasm to exploit opportunities;
- their morale.

This can be done simply and informally at the end of the business discussion. Typically the manager might ask: 'Well, George, how are things? Anything worrying you? By the way would you still be interested in that possible trip to Vancouver on the new contract?' etc.

The manager's ability to sniff out an incipient problem on these occasions is a fundamental part of his armoury of skills. People are often reluctant to open up about their real worries at work, but these formal contacts often can be turned to mutual advantage by a sensitive and personal touch.

The same principles apply to meetings, although the manager can't ask a meeting how it's feeling! Checking afterwards with individual participants is a good idea and is almost always helpful in improving the effectiveness of the next occasion. However the manager should avoid giving members a golden opportunity to criticise or gossip about one another!

Informal contacts

There is much to be said for the manager regularly 'wandering' among his staff for an informal chat. The manager being seen in the workplace is usually good for morale, but should not be overdone since it can suggest over-supervision. The personal contact forms a valuable part of staff relations.

Similar opportunities occur on social occasions – parties, outings, trips away from the workplace and the like – although the manager should take care to allow for the nature of event when weighing the value of the information he receives. Every team has at least one person who, after a couple of drinks, will tell the manager, in detail, how to run the organisation!

Appraisals

The formal appraisal of a person's progress in an organisation is a 'must' whatever the role of the employee. These should be held at least once a year and should contain a significant contribution from the employee himself. Appraisals which are simply a litany of congratulation or criticism handed down by the manager are usually of little value. The purposes of any appraisal should be for:

- the subordinate to assess his own strengths and weaknesses, progress on the work he has done and his assessment of future priorities;
- the manager to comment on the subordinate's assessment and to add his own observations or any other factor which he sees as relevant to the success of the subordinate;
- them both to agree on what can be done in terms of training, personal development, changing the job and so on.

Even the smallest organisation should have an appraisal system however rudimentary. It is an invaluable means of strengthening the bonds between the organisation and the employee, making each person consider his own function and recognising the value of the contribution of the individual to the common weal.

Responding to changing needs

The manager can only respond to needs within the limits of his own authority. However, he should always do his utmost to deal with any personal problem in his own team.

For example, a subordinate may need special training beyond the manager's budget, or be ready for a transfer elsewhere in the organisation or be facing a personal financial crisis only soluble by means of a loan from the company. In such cases the manager who shrugs off the problem with, 'Nothing to do with me' damages the relationship with the individual and the goodwill of the team.

If the changing need is one of the morale of the group – for example, dissatisfaction with salary increases or working conditions – a different response is needed. The manager's first duty is to analyse and assess the state of the problem – probably by collecting information informally – and to report it upwards through the management hierarchy. His responsibility to his team is to acknowledge the difficulty but not to react too quickly or energetically to it. Rash promises or over enthusiasm to right wrongs often prove to be no more than further causes of morale problems later. The manager's subsequent handling of it (whether by having to explain the decision from the perspective of the whole organisation, or to announce a change) should be sufficient to restore confidence. Needless to say there is a limit to the number of times a manager can get support from this team for unpalatable or foolish decisions. The manager asked to support bad management needs to consider his own future before reaching that point.

Measuring individual performance

The manager holds the key to the destiny of each of his subordinates as long as they work for him. This is particularly evident in small, close-knit companies with a dominant proprietor. It is vitally important that the judgement of that person on the performance of each individual should be consistent and fair. Where the output from the job is easily measured and jobs are generally similar there is at least some basis for a system of performance appraisal. In an increasing number of jobs, however, what constitutes acceptable performance is extremely difficult to define. How should the manager tackle this?

He should consider two factors:

- what part of the manager's task does the subordinate's task represent;
- by what criteria should the individual's task be measured?

The first of these makes the manager think about the job concerned in relation to the work of his whole team. For example, the supervisor of a section of a production line knows that the work of the whole unit is dependent equally on each element. The team requirement is therefore for the individual to maintain the same pace as everyone else, to minimise errors and failure, and to be conscientious in supporting the team effort. However, a team of salesmen rewarded largely on a commission basis has quite different performance criteria. The most powerful will be the overall achievement of sales budgets and, within that, personal targets for each salesman. Teamwork in the conventional sense will be minimal.

The manager must think through with care precisely what it is he wants from each individual job. In doing this he must separate in his mind the job from the present jobholder – perhaps by imagining what a 'perfect' employee would do.

This analysis usually forms the basis of a job description which lists the requirements of the job in order of importance. Some will be easy to measure ('Process a minimum of 200 delivery notes a day'); others won't be so easy ('Maintain good working relations with the quality assurance department'). In the last analysis all performance should be capable of measurement in terms of quality, quantity, timing or cost. The important thing is to list each item and *to explain to the jobholder* how his performance will be assessed. This can be done when the individual first takes on the role and reminders offered at appraisal meetings.

An example of part of such a briefing might go as follows:

'You'll see from the job description that the most important part of your job will be to handle quotations quickly and efficiently. Obviously, the number outstanding at any one time will vary as will their relative complexity. I would normally expect a quote to be turned around in three working days and for you to ask for help if there seems any risk of this not being practical. I expect all quotations to be double checked before coming to me for approval and I shall be watching out for this. I shall want to discuss your performance with you after your first three months. If all goes well I would hope to be recommending your appointment to the permanent staff – with a rise – at that point.'

When setting and measuring performance the manager must, of course, allow for the competence and experience of the subordinate. Setting targets unrealistically high is just as demotivating as setting them far too low. Wherever possible, targets for the team should be set and advertised and performance measured regularly against them. There is tremendous value in morale terms for aiming for and achieving a common goal. Charts on the notice board, personal bulletins and group briefings before or after working hours are usually more effective ways of reporting performance than formal management accounts or suchlike.

These methods have their dangers too. Precedents set in good times are sometimes regretted in bad. The rule is to measure and report only things which are within the control of the team and which are not, themselves, short-term phenomena. This is not to say that wider issues should not be published as part of corporate communications but they should not form a major factor in personal relations at team level.

Rewarding success

Every organisation needs an appropriate system of pay and benefits. The overall remuneration package is likely to have several components including some or all of the following:

- basic pay;
- commission or bonuses;
- profit sharing;
- share options;
- pensions;
- car or car allowance;
- medical insurance;
- life insurance cover;
- expense allowances.

How pay schemes should be organised and managed is beyond the scope of this book. However, since fair financial reward is a crucial element in getting the best out of people it is worth rehearsing the basic principles.

Pay arrangements for the organisation as a whole should:

- reflect fairly different job types in terms of grades and responsibility levels;
- be progressive by recognising increasing contributions made by individuals as they gain experience and seniority;
- be comparable with the labour market in which the organisation operates.

Maintaining fair arrangements across the organisation is a difficult task when skills vary widely and contribution to the organisation's success are hard to measure. For example, how do you compare the jobs of the hospital porter, the nurse and the surgeon? Job evaluation systems, which compare jobs on a points basis, are quite widely used, but sometimes cause more strife and bureaucracy than the results justify. In small organisations using such systems is rarely a practical proposition. In the absence of this type of measurement the market rate for a job is often the manager's most useful guide.

In judging how far the organisation should lead or follow the market in terms of pay and conditions the manager has to take into account a much wider spectrum of concerns. For example:

- does the organisation offer better or worse working conditions than its competitors?
- are training or promotion prospects better than elsewhere?
- is the content of the work more interesting or demanding than equivalent jobs elsewhere?

Being a better payer than competitors is not necessarily an attraction to potential employees or a motivator to existing staff. Being badly behind the competition is frequently a major demotivator for both potential and existing employees.

Other ways of rewarding success include:

- private and public praise on the achievements of an individual or a team;
- expanding opportunities for more interesting work, earlier promotion or enhanced training;
- prize schemes (holidays for the individual and his family are quite common – but beware the income tax pitfalls).

Of these the manager is likely to use the opportunity to praise a subordinate most frequently. Recognising a job well done is a most potent motivator. Words of praise should be used simply and sincerely avoiding extravagance and hyperbole. Public recognition is equally acceptable but care should be taken to avoid over-emphasis on individual achievement since it can affect team spirit.

Resolving conflict

The nature of human behaviour means that conflict is inevitable from time to time. Conflict involving differences in opinion resulting from genuine intellectual analysis should be encouraged by the manager. Indeed the debate which results from such conflict can be of great value both to the organisation and the maturity of the individual. However, continual conflict has an emotional and irrational content which is potentially dangerous to the organisation.

Open and continual antagonism between two individuals must be dealt with quickly and decisively by the manager. If he avoids the issue or fails to handle it successfully, his own standing as a manager will be damaged and the morale of the team considerably weakened as a result. Conflict of this sort is best resolved in private between the manager and the protagonists. The manager should seek explanations from each and ensure they recognise the adverse effects on the organisation if they continue the conflict. He should point out clearly the sanctions which will be applied should those involved not mend their ways. It is essential that the threatened penalty should not only be available to the manager but also be consistent with his normal style. To threaten to 'kick backsides to kingdom come' is neither convincing nor very clear to those involved.

On these occasions the manager must, at all costs, avoid being emotionally involved. This is very difficult and younger or less experienced managers are sometimes exploited by older and more cynical subordinates. But knowing that this is likely to happen is often half the battle.

Summary

If the manager is going to get the best out of his subordinates he must study their behaviour, both individually and as a team. He must act thoughtfully and consistently and be prepared to learn from his own mistakes. He should take every opportunity to praise good performance and to encourage greater effort. He should reprimand individuals in private and be ready to resolve conflict quickly and decisively. Above all he should *care* for his employees and share with them his own commitment to the organisation. He should keep a sense of proportion (and a sense of fun) and not strive to be super-efficient. In doing all this the manager will find not only great personal satisfaction but also the companionship which makes the most difficult problem much easier to tackle.

5

Effective Communication

Effective communication is absolutely crucial to good management. You can't get the best out of people unless you can communicate effectively with them, and they with you.

It seems easy enough. All you have to do is to tell your subordinate what you want him to do, and he gets on with it. A few words of encouragement or critisicm may be needed, but that's all there is to it. If only it were so simple! The manager has to consider three forms of communication, any of which can cause him problems if he is not careful. They are:

- oral;
- written;
- non-verbal communication.

Oral communication

Speaking directly to someone in person, by telephone or via a television link is the most common form of human communication. Oral communication is instantaneous, allows great flexibility, and permits sentiment to be combined with an intellectual message without difficulty. (Many confuse oral with verbal which literally means 'in words'; oral communications can of course be numerical.) Effective oral communication depends on a number of factors which can't always be taken for granted. These are:

- language;
- the style used;
- the supporting signals.

Language

If a manager was asked to take charge of a group of Chinese workers he would probably expect to have a language problem since everyone knows that apparently identical words can have very different meanings to people living in different countries. If, on the other hand, the group comprised his own countrymen he would assume a shared vocabulary. And in terms of ordinary words he would be right. The problem is that management includes many complicated issues which require the use of specialist words. If both parties don't share the same sense of what those words mean, the scope for misunderstanding is considerable. As a result the manager's intentions are often not fulfilled. This in turn causes him frustration and the employee confusion, and perhaps a sense of injustice.

It is not only technical or abstruse language which causes the problem; it can just as easily happen with what would otherwise seem commonplace words. Any new manager has to take particular care to explain his meaning since his predecessor might well have used words in a different way. Some examples serve to illustrate the point. The interpretations are not meant to be typical – only what can happen.

What the manager says	What he means	What the employee may *think* he means
If you have the time	I want you to do it right away	You have the choice ...
Finish it this evening	Even if you have to stay late	You have until 5.30
I'm disappointed with your work	You've got to improve or you're fired	This is a friendly hint
We shall certainly bear you in mind	You're in the running	You've got the job
We shall have to let you go	You're fired!	Take your time to look around

The list of opportunities for misunderstanding becomes immeasurably longer when meetings are involved. Managers addressing a group of staff mixed by seniority, age and sex have to tiptoe through a potential minefield of confusion. If the issues are ones of personnel management, for example, organisation, pay scales, working practices or whatever, they should take great care with the words they use.

Imagine such a meeting. The manager says 'I think we could be more efficient if we combined order checking with computer logging so I've decided to transfer Stan and Susan to Michael's section. I've asked Mike to join the executive committee and he'll take responsibility for liaison with the factory ...'

By saying, 'we could be more efficient', does he really mean that it's a shambles at the moment? If so the staff presently involved may well find it less than gratifying. The manager's decision to transfer Stan and Susan sounds like a directive which doesn't involve any sort of consultation. This may or may not be true, but the opportunity for misunderstanding is there. Mike's joining the executive sounds like good news. The likelihood is that the staff are either unsure about what its powers are or who is on it anyway. What does liaison with the factory entail? Was someone already doing the job who has been given the elbow? And so on and so forth.

Things often gets worse when questions are asked – the questioner may use 'insider' language which underlines his relationship with the manager. For example, 'Isn't it the same trouble we had with Frank Barnes?' No one else has a clue who *he* was and the manager has either to ask the questioner to explain what he means or pass on quickly leaving an air of mystery in his wake. Questioners often use meetings to make implicit political points about the organisation and their own position within it. Some use the opportunity to score points off the manager – if he allows it.

Whether the meeting is face to face or in a group, the manager has to bear three principles in mind:

- he should always be prepared to explain what he means if he has any reason to suspect that he's being misunderstood;
- he should always be in control of the communication process when dealing with subordinates and determine the vocabulary to be used;
- he should strive to make his own use of language as clear and unequivocal as possible.

Telephone calls
These too can hold pitfalls because:

- you don't know what the other person is doing (or who he is with);
- you can't see his facial expression;
- it's very easy to mis-hear what he has said.

There are few things worse than giving instructions on a conference phone. Not only is the voice disembodied, but the person receiving the call will suspect that it is being overheard. This discourages open response and mumbled assent is often the only reaction the caller receives.

Obviously, a good deal of man management is conducted on the telephone. Here are some simple rules which it is sound for a manager to follow:

- Be friendly – the recipient doesn't know if you're pleased or angry with him so put him at his ease straight away;
- Be clear – explain the purpose of your call including your instructions (if there are any) before asking for comment. This gives the recipient time to assimilate the whole message and not waste time by digressing;
- Confirm that the message is understood – this is essential because words can become garbled very easily. 'Offer them 15 per cent discount' can easily become 'Offer them 50 per cent discount';
- Listen carefully to the recipient's comments – ask for them to be repeated if you haven't wholly understood them;
- Close cheerfully – however miserable you may feel your instructions are more likely to be implemented if you are cheerful and encouraging.

Choice of style

We are often unaware of the way we say things – the language we use, the emphasis we give to certain issues and the emotional overtones involved. Transaction analysis offers some useful insight into the question of style.

Transaction analysis is the study of conversations. Research into this subject has shown that anyone's contribution to a conversation can be classified into one of three styles.

The speaker can speak as a *parent* would speak to a child. We are all familiar with the way mum or dad reassures the child with generalisations without explanations. For example, the parent may say, 'Don't speak to strangers.' If the child says, 'Why' the parent will probably reply, 'Because I say so' or 'Because it's bad.' In more mature conversations, parental statements are equally general. For example, 'The unemployed might make an effort rather than idling about' or 'Things were different in my day. We really knew how to handle blacklegs!'

A speaker may speak as a a *child* seeking reassurance from the parent. This doesn't mean he uses childish language, but that the relationship implied by what the speaker says is that of a child to a parent. For example, an employee might say, 'They're always keeping us in the dark about company policy. Why don't they do something about it?' or 'Nobody appreciates what I do for the organisation!' This style of speaking is very common in staff meetings and other occasions when personnel issues are dealt with.

The last style is the *adult* style when the speaker is conveying an unemotional message and expecting a calm and unemotional response. Most transactions should take place in this style and it should be the manager's aim to communicate in this way with his staff.

Clear transactions

These three styles can be illustrated by three interlocking circles and the speaker in any conversation may move from one style to another in the course of a few minutes. If the other person knows and responds in the appropriate style the transaction is clear.

Here are some examples:

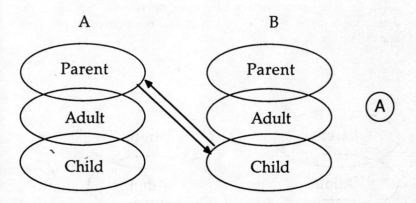

Figure 5.1

Child (B) 'I seem to be getting nowhere with the project – everything that could go wrong has gone wrong!'
Parent (A) 'Don't worry, You're doing a terrific job and I'm sure you'll sort it out'.

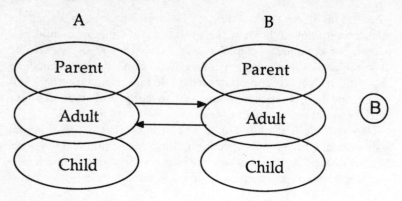

Figure 5.2

Adult (A) 'The production figures last week were down 3 per cent on the previous year. What do you think the problem was?'
Adult (B) 'The factory had to close early on Tuesday because of the maintenance inspection. I'll check what that meant in terms of output and call you back.'

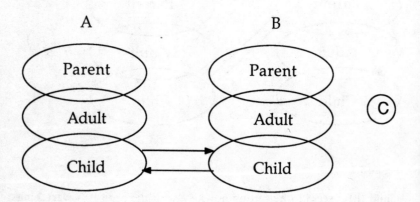

Figure 5.3

Child (A) 'When are those so-and-sos in head office going to get their fingers out and authorise the new computer.'
Child (B) 'Don't ask me old boy – I despair of that lot.'

Each of these conversations are satisfactory from both parties' point of view because the transaction is based on each subsequently understanding, and responding to, the style of the other. The manager may use the parent/child approach for some personnel issues which have an emotional content for the staff member.

Crossed transactions
Crossed transactions are the ones which cause the problems. For example:

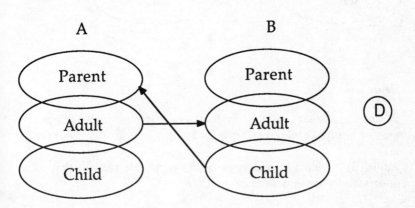

Figure 5.4

Adult (A) 'Could you find time to complete the sales stats by lunchtime tomorrow – the chairman wants a special meeting in the afternoon?'
Child (B) 'That's typical of the way we're treated around here! No consideration for how *I* feel about working late!'

At this point an argument starts which neither can win so long as the lines of communication are *crossed*. All the manager can do is to move from the adult style to the parent style and to calm the aggrieved employee. When the employee is ready to communicate as an adult, the real question – how to rearrange work to fit the new deadline – can be discussed.

Another example of crossed transaction could be:

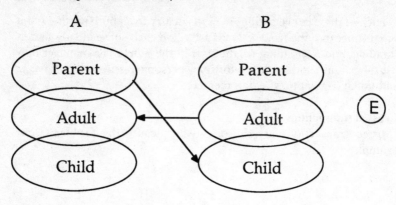

Figure 5.5

Parent (A) 'What we need is total commitment to the corporate mission – anyone who won't give us 100 per cent loyalty is not one of us.'
Adult (B) 'Could I have a copy of the corporate plan so that I can understand what that means in practice?'

More scope for argument! There are plenty of examples of crossed transactions in domestic as well as in working life. Everyone has experienced them from time to time. Some people seem to specialise in promoting them.

The message for the manager is to spot a potentially crossed transaction as early as possible and to either:

- abort the conversation until it can be put on a clear footing; or
- change his own style to make sure that communication is effective.

Supporting signals

People not only listen to what others say but also watch the gestures the speaker makes. Facial expressions are an important part of understanding what someone says, but so is the body posture.

Try saying 'come here' to someone while holding up your hand in a 'halt' gesture. The person is more likely to obey the gesture than the words. Try congratulating someone and frowning at the same time. They will almost certainly feel uncomfortable about your motives. Try telling someone to calm down while pacing up and down and wringing your hands. Their anxiety will increase rather than reduce.

The manager should match the gesture to the words. Sometimes it is impossible to disguise his underlying feeling. It is better then to share those feelings with the employee than to create uncertainty by speaking and behaving in a confusing way.

Written communication

Communication in writing should have the advantage of clarity since the writer has the opportunity to marshal his facts, present his case and make a clear recommendation. Also several people can be communicated with simultaneously, particularly in this age of electronic mailboxes and the fax machine.

In the context of man management, however, there are pitfalls which should be avoided.

Instructions can often be given more clearly in writing than orally. Remember that the recipient lacks the opportunity to question the manager directly and it is very easy for a feeling of authoritarianism to creep in. 'Give me an analysis of the sales figures for May, broken down by product and customer type,' may be unequivocal, but it can sound like a military order and the employee receiving the memorandum might be forgiven for assuming a crispness that was unintended. Small organisations use fewer internal memoranda to give instructions than large companies, and everyone probably benefits from the smaller amount of paperwork and the greater informality involved. If instructions are given at a meeting, it is always good practice to confirm the main points in writing afterwards, whatever the size of the organisation.

Personnel issues are also better dealt with orally with subsequent accurate confirmation in writing. Pay rises, promotions, changes in job specifications and the like, should not be communicated initially in writing, however good the news for the employee. Face-to-face meetings reinforce the relationship with the employee and should always be used.

Disciplinary matters are sometimes dealt with in writing because the manager is reluctant to confront the employee. This practice is always wrong and will breed misunderstanding and resentment. It is even worse when the memorandum is copied to others not directly concerned with the employee's welfare. If, for example, someone in another part of the organisation complains about an employee's efficiency or behaviour it is tempting for the manager to kill two birds with one stone. A memo of apology copied to the employee may placate the complainant, but will almost certainly infuriate the employee. If the manager needs to respond to the complaint in writing he must see the employee first and ideally show him the draft memorandum before sending it off.

Noticeboards offer a valuable means of keeping a team up to date with relevant personnel developments. The language used should, however, always be chosen with care. For example, a notice which simply says, 'Joe Smith is leaving us after four years service' is doubtless factually correct, but offers endless scope for different interpretations. Did he fall or was he pushed? Are they glad to see the back of him or is he grieved over? The addition of the word 'valuable' before 'service' and the phrase 'and we wish him well in his future career' could resolve all doubt.

Copies of memos and letters should only be sent to those who have a relevant interest in the matter in hand. Sending a copy of a memo to the recipient's superior 'for information' is usually flagrant politicking and should be discouraged. Ease of copy-making unfortunately encourages widening the audience for memos well beyond the bounds of common sense. Since recipients often feel honour bound to keep the copies they receive, the real cost to the organisation can be enormous.

Letters written to employees should always conform to the style normally used by his manager. Thus if the employee is 'John' to him, letters addressing him as 'Dear Mr Smith', 'Dear Smith', or 'Dear Sir' should always be avoided. It is part of the good manager's task to make sure that all communications with employees reinforce the organisations normal style, whether formal or informal.

Non-verbal communication

Most people are familiar with the theory of body language. The subconscious postures we adopt owe a great deal to the primitive instincts which underlie human nature.

Body language has a powerful role to play in getting the best out of people, simply because many of the circumstances in which manager and employee meet are potentially tense and artificial.

Interviews are a good example of situations which can be stressful for both people involved. Sitting behind a desk may signal a reinforcement of the manager's authority, but it usually makes the interviewee far from relaxed. It is usually better to sit with the interviewee and to avoid postures which could tend to intimidate him.

In *meetings* involving several people, signs to watch for are people sitting back from the table (showing disengagement from the group) putting hands behind their head (a subconscious gesture of aggression) or regularly stroking their hair (a signal of dissent). The manager should sit forward (showing attention) and seek regular eye-contact with each member of the group. Always looking away or staring at one's papers and avoiding eye-contact is a very powerful signal of insecurity or insincerity.

When *walking* through the work area, the manager should be aware of the potential effect of 'stalking' (looking out for trouble) or 'drifting' (unpredictable and hence, worrying). In the work area employees appreciate regular routines, for example, the manager walking the floor twice a day. The regularity and predictability of the habit is reassuring and the style with which it is done should have the same objective.

Obviously each person has his own style of gestures, walking and sitting postures. It would be foolish to suggest that anyone should radically change what is natural for them simply because it might aid the communication process. However, the employee will always look for body language signals whether the manager likes it nor not. If the manager habitually smiles, his frown will signal very bad news, and vice versa. Punctuating conversations with extravagant hand gestures may be an amusing eccentricity in small doses, but could be very distracting to long-term communications. The message for the manager is to watch for his own non-verbal signals, not only to make best use of them but also better to understand those of his staff.

Getting the best out of communication

The key component in all communication is the trust and understanding which is built up through face-to-face conversations. Telephone conversations are necessary but less effective, and written communications have many pitfalls for the unwary. The manager needs to use all three forms with skills which may not come naturally to him. Training in interviewing, chairing meetings, effective speaking and effective writing is readily available. Even in the smallest organisations, an investment in this branch of training is always soundly made.

6

The Ethics of Managing People

The hidden agenda

Ethics is not a subject which is discussed regularly or widely in most organisations. And yet the position which the enterprise takes on ethical issues, from its trading policies to it attitude towards women, affects everything it does. This hidden agenda of policies, attitudes and practice can be a minefield for the manager. Apart from the extreme cases in which the organisation is knowingly flouting the law, the issues involved are likely to be messy, inconclusive and troublesome. In young businesses the strains these problems create can prove disastrous. The manager must address those issues relevant to his management role, whether or not they have been debated more widely in the organisation for which he works.

Relevant issues

In developed countries laws tend either to be permissive (protecting our freedom to do things) or prohibitive (stopping us doing things). An example of permissive law is company legislation which protects a shareholder from unlimited liability so long as certain rules are followed. An example of prohibitive law is most tax legislation which specifies what individuals and companies may not do without paying tax. Employment law, which provides the framework within which both management and staff operate, is a mixture of the two types. Every full-time employee is required to have a contract of employment, but the terms of contract itself are a matter wholly for agreement between the parties. By comparison, trades union legislation prohibits activities such as flying pickets.

It is the job of every organisation and manager within it, to know what legislation is relevant to their enterprise and to ensure that everything they do is consistent with it. This is often difficult for the small company which has more urgent business priorities. Never the less, ignorance of the law is no defence when problems occur. Even the smallest team should include someone with a general remit to keep an eye on relevant legal requirements and ensuring compliance with them. Chambers of Commerce, Law Advice Centres and the company lawyer are all potentially valuable sources of external advice when needed.

For the purpose of this book, compliance with the law is assumed to exist. The issues relevant to the manager's ethical problems in getting the best out of the people reporting to him occur within that framework rather than outside it.

The main issues are:

- towards whom is the manager's first loyalty?
- how far is the manager discriminating in his behaviour against any group of people?
- how should the manager react when the behaviour of the organisation (or other managers) strays seriously over ethical boundaries?

First loyalties

Every individual has a series of loyalties which, ideally, are in harmony with each other. This chain of loyalties include those towards:

- his own principles and standards;
- his family;
- his organisation, whether or not it is a commercial enterprise in the strict sense;
- his friends, his community and society at large.

The individual's own set of standards is likely to be conditioned by many things. People's perception of what is 'right' and 'wrong' in terms of appropriate behaviour varies to a surprising degree. For example, the idea of acting primarily from self-interest is as acceptable to some as it is outrageous to others. Without question, however, the attitude of the organisation for which the person works can have a powerful influence over his own view of the world.

The culture of an organisation is often perpetuated through behaviour which conforms to some ethical archetype. Companies which hire and fire, emphasise individuality and personal reward, and rate lowly humanitarian attitudes towards employees, are recognisable in every community.

Benevolent, caring and lifetime service companies are equally easily identifiable. The great majority of organisations lie between these extremes. In this environment the individual receives, at best, indirect signals about the ethics involved in working for his company and, at worst, the evidence of conflicting and confusing experiences.

Unacceptable behaviour

If the organisation acts inconsistently or in a way which regularly conflicts with an individual's concept of what is right he has to ask himself whether his own position remains tenable. The individual's loyalty to himself can be put to the test, for example, when:

- colleagues are treated maliciously or unfairly;
- information is withheld, manipulated or misrepresented to him or his colleagues;
- promises made to individuals are regularly broken;
- actions in relation to suppliers, customers and others are taken carelessly or maliciously.

In simple words, cheating, lying and exploiting people but remaining within the law.

An example drawn from an entrepreneurial background will illustrate the moral dilemma such behaviour can cause.

Fred is a forceful, successful builder and occasional property developer. Self-taught, having started hod-carrying on a building site at the age of 16, he is determined and ruthless. He likes to be the life and soul of the party, to be admired by his staff and to be thought of as a local 'character'. He lives in a style which he finds difficult to afford and with two boys at public school and a wife who shops exclusively in Harrods he is always under financial pressure.

Stan is his right-hand man, his 'Sancho Panza', who has worked with him for many years. Stan was previously a building surveyor who fell out with a local firm of chartered surveyors after a dispute over a promised rise, and he has followed Fred faithfully from deal to deal for seven years. Stan has learned to keep his mouth shut and his eyes half closed when Fred is in full flight.

He knows that Fred cuts corners, delivers the odd 'present' to the district planner, and is none too scrupulous about the truth. He accepts that keeping company with Fred doesn't always win him great respect in the community. But there are compensations – the excitement of putting one over the professionals, the companionship of a strong-minded colleague and, of course, the money.

Stan does not need to address his own ethical standards or those of Fred simply because their way of business life has a set of conventions which they both understand and observe. The staff working for them are seldom involved in the rough and tumble of doing deals. Their job is to do as they are told, even if it involves 'accidentally' bulldozing a listed building or forgetting to use the high density loft insulation specified on the plans.

Fred decides to bring Philip, his son-in-law, into the business to run the office. Philip has a degree in business studies and two years' experience as a management trainee with a pharmaceutical company. He is intelligent, quiet and rather shy. At first Fred and Stan are pleased to have someone to handle the paperwork. However, Philip grows progressively more uneasy about what he sees of the way the business is run. He sees tenders being re-submitted with prices remarkably close to competitors', sub-contractors' invoices containing quantities of unexplained 'extras', and Fred and Stan drawing freely from the petty cash. His tentative expressions of concern are brushed aside by both his bosses who say that, 'he has a lot to learn about the real world'. But Philip has an enquiring mind and is not easily put off. After a couple of months he confronts Stan (after all Fred *is* his father-in-law) and demands to know what exactly is going on. Stan finds himself in a rather tight corner.

Stan has to ask himself where his own loyalty lies – with Fred (for whom he has admiration if not respect) or with Philip (a young man embarking on his career)? Should he continue the pretence that all is well, or warn Philip to opt out while he can? How far can he trust Philip not to destroy his own relationship with Fred if he tells all he knows? Stan, of course, is less likely to see these issues as problems of personal ethics than ones of practical priorities. He is used to the business of taking risks and what he decides to do is to gamble on keeping Philip quiet by admitting minor errors while continuing to conceal more major sins. But Philip is persistent. He presses on until a full scale confrontation with Fred and Stan is inevitable.

Fred has the worst problem. He regards his style as sharp rather than criminal, but he can't be sure of this. Stan, as his lieutenant, knows enough to make life very uncomfortable for him and he must avoid alienating him if he can. Philip is a member of the family but is also an employee. His idea of morality is clearly quite different from Fred's, and the prospects of their getting on together look gloomy – even if they can sort out the short term crisis.

In the event, Fred advises Philip to find a more suitable post elsewhere ('I really can't offer you the same scope as a big company'). Fred and Stan talk openly and realistically for the first time about their business ethics. They recognise what Philip did could also be done by any intelligent employee and that the time has come to operate in a rather more circumspect way. Fred even has to tell his wife that her days of shopping at Harrods are over!

Whether or not any of the characters in this example deserve sympathy is arguable. The situation they found themselves in is not, however, far removed from real life. The involvement of a new and different approach from the normal culture of a business is often the catalyst which creates the need to address moral standards. Employment and personal relationships are often so intermingled in small businesses that resolving such issues is often seen as less about principles than about individuals. In truth, many businesses which are large and successful today have faced similar, apparently crippling, dilemmas at early stages in their history. The trick is to use the opportunity they present to examine the underlying problem, and put *that* right rather than tinker with the symptoms.

Whatever the case, the principle remains the same. If the individual's loyalty to his own set of values is overstrained, it can become a matter of whether he:

- attempts to change the culture of the organisation; or
- resigns and moves elsewhere.

Usually the threat to an individual's values builds up over a period of time. Frequently small events accumulate into a personal crisis of confidence in the organisation. During that period the agony of doubt for the person concerned can be extreme. For example, if the 'custom' of the organisation is for everyone to overclaim expenses by, say, 10 per cent as a tax-free perk, the new employee has a problem. He can opt out of the system ('So who's this goody goody?'), opt in and keep his mouth shut, or blow the whistle to the tax man. If he opts in and then finds another, worrying, practice such as giving 'presents' to customers, what does he do? He can again ignore the problem and hope that something worse does not turn up. Or he can decide that a point of no return has been reached but, perhaps, only when already compromised. In the final analysis the only person who can judge is the individual himself. A manager with an uneasy conscience is certainly less likely to succeed than one at peace with his own standards.

There is no doubt that maintaining integrity is an essential characteristic of a good manager. Accepting the real world, in which compromise and occasional economy with the truth are a necessary part of achieving an objective, is equally an element in his learning process. The question is essentially one of degree. The individual's loyalty to himself and his own principles must remain intact if he is to retain the self-esteem required for high performance. Having a mature and experienced 'mentor' either inside or outside the organisation can prove invaluable when the manager needs to test his own reaction to a particular situation.

Loyalty to the organisation

What loyalty can the organisation reasonably expect from its employees? Complete support for every action it takes? Total toeing of the 'party line' both internally and externally? Or freedom to differ, debate and be outspoken about things with which the individual disagrees? The answer is that organisations get the loyalty they deserve.

Loyalty has to be earned and it is a sign of a mature organisation that it is sufficiently in tune with its employees to command loyalty on all major issues while encouraging openness on those of lesser importance. By contrast, small organisations and particularly those with a strong entrepreneurial leader are often paranoid about anything faintly 'disloyal'. Unquestioned (and unquestioning) support is the norm.

It would be ridiculous to suppose that anyone could approve of everything his organisation does. The ethical standards of the organisation should be so well understood and consistently applied, however, that the individual has to confront the question of his loyalty to it only on very rare occasions. The manager's job is to support and follow such standards with his subordinates.

A perceptive manager should also look for the ethical consequences of any major man-management decision. For example, is an action which he regards as 'fair' certain to be regarded in the same way by his staff? If not, is the manager's judgement sound, or is he applying inappropriate or out-of-date standards? Suppose his company announces a new pay structure which gives a financial advantage to married employees. Is it reasonable to wait for the unfairness to be pointed out by those affected? Will they regard it in the same way as the manager? Should he treat it as a matter of ethical principle? The more time and effort the manager puts into exploring his concerns, articulating them to his superiors and making the whole organisation sensitive to such issues the better he will serve it and himself.

In small businesses, the lack of an ethical and moral awareness of the way in which people are treated is sometimes breathtaking. Through ignorance or fear people working for powerful entrepreneurs often allow themselves to be exploited, manipulated and abused. Unless individuals are prepared to stand for consistently fair values such organisations seldom attract or retain high quality managers.

Wider loyalties

Loyalties to family, friends and the community should reflect the obligations the individual feels to those groups as complementary parts of his whole working life. Ethical problems arise when the individual is asked to behave in a way which potentially alienates him from these obligations. Part of a manager's job is to make sure that those factors do not get out of hand. He has a protective responsibility and a caring role which should be acknowledged both in what he says and what he does. His judgement of what can be asked of a subordinate is crucial to his success. If the employee's personal life is likely to be seriously and permanently affected by his work commitments, the manager must put that fact at the top of his list of priorities.

Where, then, should the individual's first loyalty lie? In the last analysis it should be towards himself and his family. A perceptive and sensitive employer will make sure that the ethical conflicts which can cause alienation do not occur. It is the individual's job to be alert to ethical problems and to report and discuss them either with his boss or someone else who can help him to decide on the right thing to do. In small companies, the entrepreneur should make sure that he sets a good example to his subordinates. One rule for the owner and another for the staff is quite unrealistic. Dishonest or devious bosses tend to be quite properly distrusted by their subordinates. They should ask themselves what advantage is really gained by putting their employees under ethical pressure. Good people will always eventually leave rather than put up with such régimes.

Discrimination – real and imagined

One of the most potent ethical issues affecting the individual at work is his attitude towards sex, religion and race. The manager needs to analyse his own behaviour to make sure that it has a rational basis.

The first step is to distinguish between 'real' and 'imagined' discrimination. Real discrimination involves a pattern of actions relating to how people are:

- recruited;
- appraised;
- communicated with;
- promoted;
- paid;
- generally esteemed;
- treated according to their sex, religion or race.

Imagined discrimination is an undue sensitivity to the way people are treated, resulting in over-compensation for what are otherwise innocent actions.

→ women already face distinct discrimination with organisations.

Real discrimination

The group most commonly discriminated against are women. The woman's role at work, whether as manager or subordinate, is increasingly difficult to protect from conscious or unconscious unfairness. Administrative procedures should be quite easy to keep under control. Recruitment routines – advertisements, application forms and initial screening techniques – can be checked to ensure that there is no suggestion that the job is essentially male-based. Appraisal and remuneration systems can also be monitored to make sure that discrimination is not promoted, but the real difficulty starts when people meet face-to-face.

Recruitment interviews are a good example. Unless well trained or very experienced the male interviewer can find interviewing an attractive young female applicant open to all sorts of pitfalls. If he draws attention to the woman's appearance a different element is introduced when compared with selecting a male counterpart. After all would he compliment a male applicant on the cut of his suit? If he has to make a particular effort to ignore the 'phenomenon', he runs the risk of making too harsh judgements about the woman's suitability. Similar problems can crop up at assessment interviews.

The woman involved can get very confusing messages about the attitude of the organisation as a result of those experiences. An atmosphere of discrimination is easily engendered and the feeling that women are at a disadvantage can be very hard to eradicate. It is often extremely difficult for the woman to know how to behave – treading a sensible path between coyness and stridency can be hard when provoked by male colleagues. Such provocation can range from innuendo (such as sexual suggestiveness through double entendre) to outright sexism.

It is depressing to find many activities still dominated by male attitudes and prejudice. The likelihood of a woman not having a continuous career from school to retirement is one underlying reason for such discrimination. Others lie deep in the culture of our society. For example, women are sometimes assumed to be more emotional and easily influenced than men. They are expected to have to work harder, to achieve more and to adopt a 'male' approach to succeed. Society continually offers examples of the fallacies of these beliefs. The revolution in attitudes to women which started in the western world after the First World War has already produced striking instances of women with outstanding qualities in most walks of life. It will take many years for these changes to affect all aspects of life at work. In the meantime, both working men and women face ethical problems not found elsewhere in society. What should they do?

One answer is to ignore the problem and make the best of the immediate relationships. Another is actively to seek to change the attitudes and procedures of the organisation from within. The approach adopted must suit both the circumstances and the individual. It is clear, however, that optimum personal performance is far less likely to be achieved in a climate of active discrimination than one which is fair to all employees. The reason is that both self-esteem and morale are affected by the standards set by the organisation. If the organisation is generally 'in step' all will be well. If it is not, disharmony and discontent are sure to occur at some time or another.

Variety in attitudes and standards of behaviour is healthy in any organisation and, indeed, should be encouraged. It is the extreme and consistent lack of recognition of the need for equality of treatment which is corrosive to morale and devastating in terms of inefficiency.

Imagined discrimination

Some organisations seem to bend over backwards to show that they do not discriminate in their employment practices against any particular group. Their protestations often result in 'positive' discrimination; what would otherwise be the normal criteria for job selection, promotion, pay rises and the like, are suspended in favour of an overriding factor – membership of a certain group (including women). Such action may sometimes be needed in the short term to correct an employment imbalance. In the longer term it is discriminatory (and hence undesirable) to the majority group and consequently as undesirable as the attitude it seeks to replace.

Despite the dangers of overreaction it is useful for every organisation to check from time to time that it is seen to be acting both internally and externally in a way which is not discriminating. For example, if an organisation reaches a substantial size and finds itself with patterns of employment which don't reflect the structure of the community in which it works, something may be wrong. Perhaps the style, recruitment approach or employment methods do not attract applicants from minority groups such as ethnic minorities, and disabled people. Being an employer offering equality of opportunity is not just a useful recruitment aid. It adds to the diversity and richness of culture of the organisation and the contribution it can make in a wider social context.

Women managers

It is clearly hard to be a member of a minority group and to find discriminatory attitudes and actions among superiors and colleagues. It is even harder to compete and succeed in such environments as a manager.

The woman manager must not only face possible discrimination from her colleagues and superiors but must also make special efforts to be fair to her subordinates. There are some activities in which this is particularly hard, namely:

- task assignment (women managers are often assumed either to have favourites or to discriminate against men);
- assessment (women managers are believed to be more influenced by flattery, can be more easily misled, to be more emotional in their judgements and so on);
- discipline (women managers are accused of losing control, being vindictive and other equally 'non-male' behaviour traits).

The fallacies bracketed above will be immediately apparent to anyone who has worked for a good woman manager. (And bad managers are awful whatever their sex.) But the sad fact is that fewer women than men achieve managerial positions because of these prejudices.

In approaching their task as managers, women have to recognise and, where needed, compensate for, these problems. They occur surprisingly often in small organisations in which a consciousness of the need for good personnel management has been relegated to a lower status than the need to survive. The woman manager has to be particularly careful to handle the human relations aspects of her job with sensitivity. For example, it is usually easier for a male subordinate to confide domestic problems to a male than to a female boss. A good sense of humour (including the capacity to laugh at herself) is probably the best attribute a woman can have to overcome the awkwardness which often accompanies such management actions.

A typical example of this problem is the challenge a woman faces at being put in charge of a group of male colleagues for the first time. How should she establish her authority over them?

Sally is recruited by a small design company to take charge of a section of three men working on corporate identity assignments. Her qualifications are excellent, her previous experience impressive and her personal style brisk and authoritative. Her new boss, Ian, is delighted to have attracted such a high class candidate and is not concerned that Sally has had no managerial experience before. Her induction to the company consists of Ian accompanying her round the office on her first morning introducing her to her new colleagues and a half-hour session with the salary clerk dealing with the paperwork associated with her joining the firm.

She finds her desk and meets her team. Two are about her own age and one is considerably older. They give her a wary welcome and she doesn't know whether to hold an informal 'meeting' or to retire to her office and let them get on with their work. She decides to say that she's glad to be part of the team and that she 'feels sure they'll get on well together'. As she walks away conscious that she is blushing, her colleagues exchange some comments, *sotto voce*, which she is sure are not complimentary. Not a good start. She decides to call them in, one at a time, to discuss their projects with them.

Bill, the first to come in is self-confident to the point of insolence, sits on the corner of her desk and calls her 'sweetie'. The interview is short and embarrassing. The second, Ted, starts by telling that he has a daughter her age who's 'doing what all women should be doing – staying at home bringing up the kids'. Rising to the bait Sally hotly defends womens rights to equality of opportunity only to be met with a muttered, 'Women's libbers!' Discussion about Ted's project is professional and constructive but Sally has an uneasy feeling that their relationship is not going to be easy.

The last to come in is Jengha. Quiet and studious and extremely polite he seems the ideal colleague. He happily shows Sally his drawings, accepts her comments and suggestions and takes neat and complete notes. It makes it even more difficult to know how to react when he asks her out for a meal. His disappointment, if any, when she says 'no' is well concealed and he leaves her with a shrug. At lunchtime Sally finds the office deserted and has a lonely hamburger wondering whether she's done the right thing in changing jobs.

This poor beginning leads to poor management relationships. The harder Sally tries to be liked and to guide rather than direct, the more her team seem to do just what they want. When she gets cross Ted accuses her of 'female temperament', when she is cool and businesslike Bill blows her kisses and says 'She's sexy when she's cross.' Her insecurity about her ability as a manager gets inextricably confused with her feeling of being picked on because she's a woman. The more she tries to compensate for what she feels are her weaknesses, the more she seems to feed their prejudice.

Sally gets little guidance or support from her boss who is an extremely busy man. She has no management training and has no-one to turn to for help. And yet many of the problems could have been avoided with a little forethought and preparation. She could have:

- thought about her management responsibilities and been prepared to explain them to her team on first meeting them;
- decided how she was going to work and explained it to her colleagues;
- anticipated the likelihood of prejudiced treatment and been prepared to deal with it before it occurred.

This last point is the one most germane to the ethical issue. She could say 'I know its probably a bit of a novelty for you to be working for a woman, but I promise you I'll do my best just to be a good manager. In a week or two you'll regard me as just another colleague. In the meantime I hope we can avoid the old jokes about 'a woman's place' and so on. Now to business ….'

Male colleagues are probably more ready to exploit weakness in a women manager than they are of other men in the organisation. It is tempting for the woman to compensate by being both unduly meticulous and sensitive to potential criticism. Some go further by dressing and behaving in a masculine way. Women undoubtedly need to show both competence and confidence in their jobs, but this is true of all managers. The capable woman manager should also express her femininity in uncompromising ways. Differences between the sexes should be a source of mutual reassurance in the process of managing people, rather than a diversion from it. In small companies, the informality which epitomises relationships between people should encourage women to make their best possible contribution. After all the family is the context in which women often enjoy the most esteem. Good companies echo this family feeling.

TASC LIBRARY LRS

Organisations over the top

Sometimes individuals find themselves in real ethical dilemmas because the organisation for which they work behave in a way which seriously conflicts with their own standards. Here are some examples:

- The organisation may employ dubious methods to obtain business such as 'backhanders', unnecessarily lavish entertaining, or industrial espionage. Such activities may be well known in the organisation, but not provable by the individual.
- The organisation may have a culture of untruthfulness – perhaps not in major matters – but lying about delivery dates, sales figures and pay rates, and 'fiddling the firm' or whatever is the norm rather than the exception.
- The organisation may exploit weakness – either at individual level in the way it treats an employee or groups such as suppliers, non-unionised employees, its pensioners and so on.

There are many instances in which the individual feels uncomfortable when faced with a lack of moral values in his employer. No organisation is so scrupulous in its behaviour that aberrations will never occur, and most employees recognise and allow for this. If the fault is consistent it can progressively erode the values of the individual, often without his realising it. It is astonishingly easy, for example, to fall into the routine of over-claiming expenses (if everyone seems to do it) or to knock off half an hour early if unsupervised. The habits formed in this way particularly in the early years of one's working life can be very hard to change. In small companies it is difficult for an individual not to comply with the culture and the best route is probably escape to another organisation. In any event, the individual should take up his disquiet with his manager before deciding what to do.

The manager is in a tough position too. He has to take care that his own reputation and career are not prejudiced by having been involved in an organisation with low standards. But he has another problem – supporting management decisions with which he disagrees.

Normally the manager's job is to explain and apply the decisions made by his superiors. The judgement the manager makes about revealing his own views and concern about the rightness of a particular decision will depend on:

- his relationship with his team;
- the 'normal' pattern of agreement and support for such decisions in the past;

- the morale of the team and the organisation as a whole.

If the decision is ethically outrageous in the manager's eyes – for example if it deals grossly unfairly with a group or an individual employee – he may find himself unable to support the decision at all. In such cases there is only one correct course – to inform his boss and to resign his position. Anything less will not only compromise the manager's standards in his own eyes but also in those of his team. This can be a fatal blow to the subtle and very personal relationships which must exist for the manager to achieve the best results from his subordinate's work.

When the chips are down

Ethical standards are often lower in organisations because individuals do not speak up as often as they should about the disquiet caused them. Standards cannot be absolute and each person will set different criteria by which 'good' and 'bad' behaviour should be judged. Despite this, managers have an important responsibility to monitor and guide the standards of their own staff. In addition they must comment on the morals of the organisation at large and be prepared to resign their jobs if the behaviour is persistent and extreme.

Standards of ethics and morals can change – sometimes quite rapidly. Practices which by custom have been acceptable for years can suddenly be found to be beyond the pale. The rapid change in attitudes towards the acceptability of insider dealing is a good example of this. Similarly, attitudes towards the compatibility of homosexuality with holding positions of authority are changing. In an ideal world, every employer would be in step with these processes. In practice, organisations are either ahead of the social norms or behind them. Every employee can contribute towards helping those who are tardy.

Discrimination exists everywhere, but its manifestation in employment is more obvious and potentially damaging than anywhere else in society. The dangers of overcompensation for imagined discrimination are almost as severe as the real thing. Women are in a particularly difficult position as managers and have to recognise the likelihood of male prejudice in many organisations. Organisations which are well led, whether small or large, actively support the role of women in their work. They recognise that there are differences between the sexes (it would be daft to do otherwise) but recruit, appraise, promote and pay on the really relevant criteria – excellence in the job. When the chips are down, a woman working in an organisation which fails to recognise this necessity can either work to change the system or leave for a more promising job elsewhere. Sadly one of these options is all too commonly necessary.

competitive advantage.

See page 115

7

Only the Best Will Do

A venture in common

Getting the best out of people involves making a bargain. The manager commits himself to fairness, consistency, supporting his staff and helping them to fulfil their potential. In return the subordinate offers loyalty, enthusiasm and hard work.

At the same time, the manager must attempt to get the best out of himself. He should be learning all the time both in the techniques of management and from practical experience. His imperfections will undoubtedly be apparent to his staff in much the same way that theirs are to him. Ideally, manager and staff will learn from each other, building up a long-term bond of mutual respect and understanding.

The strength of the bond can be indicated by:

- team spirit;
- morale;
- loyalty to the manager;
- flexibility in the face of change;
- friendship.

Team spirit. A good team works together. Members of the team will support and help each other, will cooperate with other groups, and will recognise and respect each individual's contribution to the whole. The best analogy is a well managed football team, working together towards a common purpose which is well understood and sought after.

Poor team spirit is indicated by individuals 'looking after number one', fighting over working arrangements (however trivial) and disarray in the face of any threat to the unity of the team. If poor team spirit exists, then a thorough and open review with the whole team followed by positive corrective action may be the only cure. This may need to include changing the manager.

Morale can be measured by the degree of dedication to the work in hand, cheerfulness and enthusiasm, and the willingness to contribute to the team effort. The 'easy' working relationship between a good manager and his staff, in which communication appears effortless and natural is underpinned by mutual respect. 'No go' areas are mutually understood, and neither party crosses these unwritten boundaries even under the severest provocation. But the team are likely to be able to offer constructive criticism and comments to their managers because each understands and respects the other's role.

Poor morale is usually a direct consequence of poor management. The process of rebuilding poor morale is normally slow and painstaking – distrust of management leaves a scar and confidence can only be restored through consistent action over a sufficiently long period.

Loyalty to the manager can be judged by the extent to which his staff will follow his leadership and defend him against criticism. A manager gets the loyalty he deserves – it will only be earned through good management techniques, consistent and sound judgement, and team obligation. Standing up for the team in the face of senior management pressure is a typical action which wins team loyalty.

The manager who earns the loyalty of his staff should also be prepared to deal severely with those who fail to support his role. If team spirit is good such action will be approved by the rest of his staff; but if he fails to deal with disloyal behaviour, team morale could be damaged.

Flexibility is essential to efficient man-management. The manager must frequently reassign tasks within the team to accommodate changing patterns of work demand and the level of individual's skills. External factors also play a part. For example, new procedures or processes involving high technology can revolutionise individuals' jobs. A well managed team are more likely to accept and support the need for change and trust the manager's judgement on how it should be handled. If this trust does not exist a reluctance to change, probably caused by fear, will soon become apparent.

Friendship between the manager and his team is often either discounted or totally ignored as a factor in achieving high performance. In practice, comradeship (rather than 'mateyness') exists in all well managed teams. Being seen as a fallible human does not necessarily expose the manager to over-familiarity or pose a threat to his authority. The manager's job and the expertise which secured his assignment to it should give him a sound basis for handling personal relationships. Sadly, many managers suffer from feelings of insecurity which result in their distancing themselves from their subordinates. This creates an atmosphere which eliminates the opportunity for developing comradeship.

The size of the organisation

The size of the organisation is irrelevant to the *principles* of good man-management. In practice however, working in a small or large organisation gives rise to different advantages and disadvantages. Good and bad points of typical companies can be classified as follows:

	Organisation size		
	Small	*Medium*	*Large*
Management training	None	Fair	Good
Development opportunities	Poor	Good	Fair/Good
Promotion opportunities	Fair/Very good	Good	Good
Formality of relationships	Very informal	Informal/Formal	Formal
Variety of activities	Wide	Limited	Narrow
Personnel support	None/Limited	Fair	Good
Importance of personal style	Very important	Fairly important	Unimportant at junior levels

Individuals who like variety, informality and a personal approach tend to be attracted towards small organisations. Those who seek security, specialist training and personal development find larger organisations more interesting. Small organisations offer more immediate opportunities for responsibility and involvement in corporate success as long as the organisation prospers. If it fails to grow successfully, the lack of opportunity for formal personal development tends to limit the individual's scope and future. Large organisations usually offer a slower development and promotion profile, but greater long-term opportunities.

Each person must choose for himself which environment is likely to offer the most satisfactory working experience. Some individuals move between different sizes of organisation to obtain a variety of exposure to management techniques. Moving from a small to a larger employer is more difficult than the reverse. If a manager is to be really effective he is likely to get better training in a large organisation than a small one; if his career plan is to specialise in management, then starting in a large company is difficult to beat.

The test of the crisis

Man-management is about being able to handle the crises – the normal course of business is the easy bit. Every manager has a horror story to tell of some event which tested both his expertise and his nerve. A few examples will help to show how valuable these are to the manager's personal development.

The drunken boss

Mr Johnson is the manager of a buying department, with a total staff of 12 people. Of these, the most senior is Bill Murgatroyd who has worked in the department for some seven years. He has worked for Mr Johnson for four years, having narrowly missed promotion when the manager was transferred from a subsidiary. The relationship between the two men is cordial and businesslike, but fairly cool. Bill respects Mr Johnson's technical skill but finds him a bit impersonal and cold. Morale in the department is adequate, but two staff have left in the last year and their replacements have taken a long time to settle down.

Over a period of some weeks Bill becomes aware that Mr Johnson is starting to hit the bottle. His behaviour after lunch each day is erratic. He is irresponsible, shuts himself off from his staff and is sometimes found asleep at his desk. Bill tries to talk about it with Mr Johnson but is told to mind his own business. The staff are beginning to make fun of the manager behind his back and discipline and enthusiasm are rapidly deteriorating. Bill has to decide what to do.

He owes loyalty to Mr Johnson (his boss) and must not be seen telling tales about him. On the other hand, he has a responsibility to the company and to his staff for the efficiency of his department. He could of course keep his head down and wait for Mr Johnson to be found out (with the prospect of the promotion he thinks he deserves).

He should correctly:

- tell Mr Johnson about his worry (as a colleague) and advise Mr Johnson to seek advice;
- watch his manager's subsequent behaviour and, if there is no change, repeat the advice with the additional comment that he, Bill, may have to report his concerns to Mr Johnson's boss (or the personnel department);
- reassure the staff that he has not only noted the problem but discussed it with Mr Johnson (Bill must be seen to support his manager in this problem);
- if no improvement occurs, report the problem to a superior as a matter of real concern about the well-being and health of a colleague.

These actions are unlikely to make Bill popular with either his boss or his staff. Popularity is less important than taking the correct management action as all good managers will testify.

The public rebuke
The same Mr Johnson (having overcome his drinking problem) singles out a junior employee for a dressing down in front of his peers. The misdemeanour is persistent lateness without (in his opinion) an adequate excuse. What are the consequences of this action?

- Mr Johnson feels a sense of satisfaction that justice has been done and has seen to be done;
- the rebuked employee feels picked on, humiliated and resentful;
- his colleagues feel embarrassed and concerned that they too might be subjected to the same treatment at some time or another.

As a result, the manager will tend to lose sympathy, team morale will fall and 'solidarity' with the victim will develop however reasonable the telling off was. Disciplinary action taken in public is very rarely effective and almost always damaging to the morale of the team.

The hare and the tortoise
In the buying department, there are two clerks carrying out similar tasks, but with very different reputations in the group. Alan is young, ambitious and self-confident. He has only worked in the department for a couple of years but has friends and admirers for his energy and bravura. He is particularly admired for his carefree attitude towards authority.

His colleague, Ken, is 15 years older than Alan. He is a steady, unadventurous person, quiet, competent and rather unambitious. Some years ago he was offered the job of section leader but turned it down on the grounds of his lack of experience. Alan and Ken get on well together, without being matey, don't argue about work and are regarded as a good team.

Mr Johnson is told that, because of changing company needs, he must dispense with the services of either Alan or Ken. The redundancy rules would suggest that Alan, with shorter service, should go first. However, Ken would get a generous severance payment. What should Mr Johnson do?

His problem is decide on the 'value' of the two employees to the organisation. Alan has great potential but is, as yet, raw and undeveloped. Ken has reached his ceiling but has extensive experience and is deeply loyal. In assessing value Mr Johnson has to take into account the needs of:

- the department (today and tomorrow);
- the team;
- the individual.

The first might include considerations of changing technology or working methods. The second should take into account the reaction of the team to the decision (in terms of fairness to the individual and morale generally). The third considers what is best for the individuals concerned. The judgement is a complex process; the future well-being and job satisfaction of the individual retained are as important as the immediate effect on the one who is released.

In the event Mr Johnson decided to keep Ken arguing that Alan had more prospect of recovering from losing his job than Ken. When he had made his decision, he undertook to arrange development training for Ken to ensure that his career prospects with the firm were secure.

A square peg

Sally, a section leader in the department has an extremely bright junior colleague, Amanda. Amanda has not been with the department long but is already showing a remarkable capability in her job – as one of her colleagues puts it, 'she takes it at a canter!' She's been on all the training courses, learned from her colleagues and has coped with the crises and pressures that are part of the job. When conducting her appraisal, Sally is keenly aware that Amanda is too good for the job she is being asked to do. But she seems content, hasn't pressed for promotion or more pay, and is cheerful and well liked.

Sally assesses her options as follows. She could:

- leave Amanda in her present job and do nothing until she demands it – that way she'll have an extremely valuable subordinate and a happy team;
- recommend her for promotion – this would need to involve a transfer to another department since the next job in the hierarchy in the department would be Sally's own, so she would lose her most able subordinate but the organisation as a whole would benefit from Amanda's potential being realised elsewhere;
- reorganise the jobs in her section to give Amanda more responsibility and opportunity to develop – this would keep her in the team but could adversely affect the jobs of her colleagues.

Of these possibilities, the first is the worst (although most commonly chosen) because Sally would be failing in her responsibility to Amanda. The second choice is usually the best (assuming a suitable place exists) because the benefit to the organisation and the goodwill Sally will generate for caring unselfishly for her staff's careers outweighs the disadvantages. The third is attractive in the short term as a stepping stone to the second. A good manager is consistently on the look out for ways in which he can 'enrich' the jobs done by his staff. Adding responsibility, variety, interest to the task to reflect the developing capabilities of the individual should be an automatic response to their changing needs.

Square pegs in round holes are quickly detected by colleagues (particularly if the square peg is a manager!) and a persistent misfit will eventually weaken team effectiveness. A square peg who is *too* competent is as big a problem as one who is incompetent. Individuals are often able to set their own goals, judge their own competence and suggest the best way for their careers to develop. Very often they are not even asked for that opinion!

Lessons for the manager

A manager has to tackle a wide range of human problems of varying complexity. His success in solving these problems will determine his own future achievement as a manager. Unless the manager sets himself standards his approach can easily slide from the best to the merely acceptable. Above all he has to take account of the individuality of everyone working for and with him, and be aware of his own strengths and weaknesses.

The lessons to learn are legion. It is an unending process and even the most experienced managers will agree that they are still learning on the day they retire!

Managing people – some principles

Although there are no hard and fast rules for managing people, there are some guiding principles it would be wise to follow.

- *Consistency*. However experienced a manager is, consistency is an essential quality. Everyone needs a framework of reasonable certainty about the way they will be treated. The manager should always strive to be consistent and, when his approach changes, should explain why and how to those affected.
- *Fairness*. The manager's job is a balancing act between conflicting demands and loyalties. He also has to cope with the ethics of his own role and his responsibility for others. No one can be fair all the time, but it is always worthwhile examining any major management decision from all relevant perspectives.
- *Leadership*. Even the most junior manager improves his performance if he shows style, individuality and a sense of humour. In the words of a famous general, 'His troops would follow him anywhere ... if only out of curiosity!'
- *Observation*. The manager should listen, watch and remember the personalities, attitudes and concerns of those for whom he is responsible. Occasional remarks dropped into a conversation may well indicate problems which would otherwise go unrecognised. Caring for staff does not mean softness or interfering, it is a vital part of the job.
- *Confidence*. Even though the manager may feel insecure or diffident, he should not transmit these emotions to his staff. Confidence is not necessarily shown by bombast or aggressiveness; it can be conveyed equally well by a quiet and measured manner.
- *Communication*. It is vital that the manager communicates his decisions clearly and unequivocally – there are few things worse than a manager whose briefings are vague or wandering. If you emerge from a meeting unclear about who is to do what, by when and with what resources, communications have failed.

- *Effort*. The manager must show a clear example to his staff by working hard at his own job. Any lack of commitment to his role or failure to attend to the needs of his team, will be quickly detected.

- *Friendliness*. The manager should be approachable, humane and show an interest in the lives of his staff. If he is natural, convivial and can occasionally socialise with his staff, the morale of the team will undoubtedly be improved. False bonhomie or artificially being 'one of the boys' is, however, counterproductive.

- *Directness*. When praise for good performance or censure for poor performance is called for, the manager should use simple, direct and appropriate language. It is easy to appear insincere in congratulating someone if the approach is too fulsome. Equally, endless repetition of disappointment at someone's failure will irritate and demoralise rather than encourage improvement. Most people are more severe in their self-criticism than any management stricture would suggest, and a few well chosen words of concern are often quite sufficient.

- *Self-respect*. The manager must not only earn the respect of his team, but must feel that he is acting in a proper and appropriate way. If he faces a serious problem of business or personal ethics, he must make his judgement of what to do with this factor clearly in mind. A manager with a guilty conscience is unlikely to enjoy good relations with his staff.

- *Self-awareness*. Everyone has imperfections and the mature manager not only recognises his own but allows for them in the way he behaves. If he is likely, for example, to allow his emotions to interfere with his judgement when handling a personnel problem he should seek support and corroboration from a colleague when such situations arise. The ability to laugh at one's own weaknesses is regarded by most people as showing strength of character and is a lesson which the manager does well to remember.

- *Failure*. A manager can learn as much from failure as from success. It is as necessary a part of his own development as it is of his staff. A healthy understanding of this, and an indomitable attitude towards building success out of reverses are commendable qualities in a good man manager. Every potential manager must also be given the opportunity to fail and not be overprotected.

Getting the best out of people

Striving to be a good manager should brook no compromise. Only the best should do, both in his personal behaviour and the expertise with which he handles his colleagues. It is a demanding task, but the effort will be rewarded by personal satisfaction and managerial success.

Further reading

The following list contains books and articles which have either already stood the test of time or promise to do so. There are plenty of other publications which contain valuable insights into personnel management issues. In gaining a better understanding of the complex world of work in which we live the reader is encouraged to forage widely, but critically.

Management, Peter F Drucker, Pan, 1979

High Output Management, Andrew S Grove, Souvenir Press, 1984

The Experienced Manager, John Humble, McGraw-Hill, 1973

Management Methods, D Torrington, J Weightman and K Jones, Institute of Personnel Management, 1985

'One More Time: "How Do You Motivate Employees?"', Fred Herzberg, Harvard Business Review, Jan/Feb 1968

Motivation and Personality, A H Maslow, Harper and Row (New York), 1954

I'm OK, You're OK, Thomas A Harris, Pan, 1973

Women in Charge, Aileen Jacobson, Van Nostrand Reinhold, 1985

In Search of Excellence, Thomas J Peters and Robert H Waterman, Harper and Row, 1983

Creating Excellence: Managing Corporate Culture Strategy and Change in the New Age, Craig Hickman and Michael Silva, Unwin Paperbacks, 1986

The Aquarian Conspiracy, Marilyn Ferguson, Paladin, 1982

The Human Organisation: its Management and Value, R L Lickert, McGraw-Hill, 1967

Books from Kogan Page

Don't Do. Delegate! The Secret Power of Successful Managers, James M Jenks and John M Kelly, 1986

Effective Interviewing, John Fletcher, 1988

Essential Management Checklists, Jeffrey P Davidson, 1987

The First-Time Manager, M J Morris, 1988

How To Be an Even Better Manager, Michael Armstrong, 1988

How to Make Meetings Work, Malcolm Peel, 1988

Profits from Improved Productivity, Fiona Halse and John Humphrey, 1988

Winning Strategies for Managing People, Robert Irwin and Rita Wolenik, 1986

Index